Copyright 2018 Elizabeth Richardson AUSTRALIA

*This book is licensed for your personal enjoyment.
We always appreciate being acknowledged when you
repost, reprint, or reuse any part of the material herein.*

Thank you for respecting the integrity of this work.

Hello. This is Elizabeth.
Elizabeth is wise.
She doesn't put a big copyright note on her stuff.
She knows that she can't really stop other people from doing whatever they want to do, unless she throws a lot of time, effort, focus and money towards preventing it.
Be wise like Elizabeth.
Believe that people respect you,
Keep on creating one step ahead,
Focus forward … and spend the money on shoes … ☺

#ThisIsElizabeth

Preface

500 Confessions has been likened to a modern-day Course in Miracles, offering a soothing, thought-provoking, and often humorous twist. It doesn't preach, instruct, or aim to teach—but it will take you on an adventure into your own life, offering an open-hearted exploration of relationships, revealing your current beliefs, and helping you choose more life-enhancing ones.

Written in a unique style, it soothes doubts, eases fears, inspires hope, and delivers plenty of laughs, all in one.

The book includes some swearing, discussions of sex, and a small amount of adult content—just like life, seen as it truly is, with a fresh perspective on how to make it even better.

Aimed at readers 25 and older, 500 Confessions appeals to those seeking practical, warm, and entertaining ways to hear their inner guidance more clearly. It's especially resonant for those who appreciate the teachings of Abraham Hicks™.

A Snippet from Book 1

I'M NOT HERE TO FIX YOU … I know you are perfect just the way you are, that you are completely worthy and no longer need to prove it, that you are loved and appreciated more than you will ever know … and when I give you space to decide what's right for you, when I trust you're receiving your own guidance too, when I accept your uniqueness is what makes life sublime, you'll find your own way too, just as I found mine. - CONFESSION #326

I CAN'T HELP YOU … there's NOTHING wrong with you. Your attention to your own perceived problems and the failing of others to help you in the way you think they should, keeps you stuck right where you are. Therapy is a way humans use to exchange money by first deciding someone else actually has a problem and then pretending they can fix it. Only YOU can change your focus and give full attention to what you desire to create instead. - CONFESSION # 35

"The words just keep getting clearer, lighter, more empowering and easier to apply."

About The Author

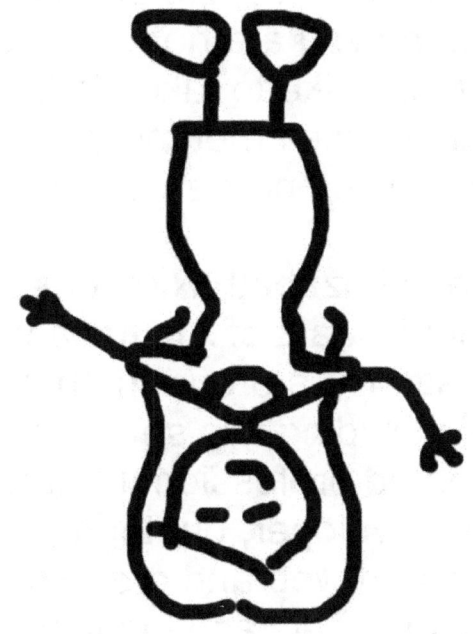

This is Elizabeth

Elizabeth lives in Australia … 😊

About The Author – Really!

Ha ha ha ha ha … Hello and welcome. I'm so happy you are here. As you can probably tell, I like to take life lightly. For those who haven't met me yet, let me introduce myself properly.

My name is Elizabeth Richardson, and I live on the Gold Coast of Australia with my two ragdoll cats. I'm a proud mother of six children, including two sets of twins. As a multi-talented professional, I work as a business developer, photographer, strategic marketer, and web and graphic designer, helping individuals and businesses bring their dreams to life.

With a rich background as a professional counsellor, group therapy leader, and well-being advocate, I've had the privilege of training with some notable experts like Robert Kiyosaki (Rich Dad Poor Dad) and Tony Robbins, honing my skills in powerful presentations and strategic intervention techniques. I am also a certified Conscious Breathing Practitioner with the Australian Institute of Rebirthing.

As the author, or co-author, of over 15 Feel Good books, I blend personal fulfillment into every aspect of my work. My life and business philosophies are deeply inspired by the teachings of Abraham-Hicks™.

These days I pretty much enjoy a life of freedom and contribute where I feel most valued and inspired. My passion for living, loving, and laughing, remains at the forefront of my focus.

Elizabeth Richardson

My Job Description

- My job is to uplift others, not to point out their weaknesses.
- My job is to turn negative perceptions into life giving ones.
- My job is to give hope where hope has been lost.
- My job is to talk about what's possible, not to agree about what others think is impossible.
- My job is to spread good news, not to regurgitate the bad.
- My job is to encourage each person's uniqueness, not to resolve differences.
- My job is to celebrate individuality, not to promote sameness.
- My job is to soothe you into loving yourself more, to inspire you to follow your own unique path, to draw out more of your phenomenal strengths, to see your magnificence reflected in the eyes of everyone else and encourage you to align with your own precious Soul.

Special Acknowledgements

I have overflowing appreciation for the teachings of Abraham-Hicks™. Just a simple 3 Step foundation is all anyone will ever need to remember. I've found untold comfort, success, freedom, prosperity, inspiration and jubilation and have cultivated a deep faith in my own innate guidance because of living this way.

Abraham says.

Step 1: Ask (Life is constantly causing us to ask for improvement).

Step 2: Source answers (It's done).

Step 3: Allow the answer/solution to be shown. Relax about it, stop asking the question or reinforcing the problem, chill out, expect what I want will be given. Have faith in the process, it works.

It's not the only way to live; it's just the way I've found to be profoundly effective for me.

I also want to extend a heartfelt thank you to all the wonderful men in my life who offer sincere compliments, allow me to be playful without expectation, and provide unwavering kindness and support. Your presence has helped me feel secure, taught me more about myself as a woman, and reminded me that I can trust my instincts again.

To all the amazing men who work hard to provide for us, who balance our feminine energy simply by being present, and who acknowledge the beauty and comfort women bring to your lives—thank you. You make us feel valued and appreciated just as we are.

Men contribute something truly special to this world—as protectors, partners, fathers, friends, and more. You forgive our moods, overlook misunderstandings, and support us even when we don't ask for help. I appreciate you deeply and can't imagine life without you.

Finally, I'd like to thank all the people who've caused trouble in my life, because you are the ones who made me expand the most, into the amazing person I am today.

What Other People Are Saying

Since the conception of "500 Confessions" directly on the pages of Facebook, it's received thousands of comments, requests and testimonials. Here's what others say.

I just read a few words and my energy is increased. You are a miracle worker. – Carol Finlayson

500 Confessions is a brilliant book on Universal Law and Principles that is fabulously written as it is short, to the point and funny. I have never laughed out loud so much and that is the way it must be. Spirituality is all about fun and laughter. Congratulations Elizabeth Richardson!!! YOU ROCK!!! - Susan M. Garcia

You are a Rare Bright and Shining, brilliant Light filled with Wisdom, Contagious Freedom, Ease and Joy. It is my pleasure to call you friend. - Carolee Dalton (God Without Guilt)

I really enjoy reading your Confessions! Sometimes they are just what I need to find insight. – Shawn Maskel

YOU are one of my greatest inspiring forces, a precious human being - Simret Jandu

I just finished studying your Confessions up to 500. Thank God. I love to read them again and again. They are instilling hope, expectation, faith, optimism and above all an attitude of 'Feeling Good' in all situations of life. - Shaukat Charania

I LOVE what you write. Every single thing speaks directly to me as I'm banging around on this new-found path. I'm so appreciative of amazing, thoughtful, bright lights (like you) reaching a hand back to help me along, even though you're scarcely aware of the tremendous impact you have on so many. Many blessings sister-friend! - Shelli Clemens

Your insights always come like speak or radiance of light whatever the size they are pristine and precise open up a space with a key. Thank you so much - Niranjan Ashok Mallapur

Your Confessions always bring me into the vortex. I just love them so much, and I love you so much. Keep confessing. I just like the feelings of 'high' your Confessions provide. – Zetty Zakaria

I love it! I start my day with 500 Confessions one or two a day just let them sink in... Thank you! - Leah Witmer-Melendez

You so eloquently capture through written word, my very thoughts and feelings. Thank you for the work you do. – Lucy Bordonaro

The most sensible words I have read on relationships. Thank you Elizabeth Richardson. Salute. Respect. - Ravie Ravan Kathuria

After 40 years of marriage my wife left me. Your beautifully expressed wisdom has helped banish the pains of the wound that caused me to run away and hide. Your exhortation to "go out and have fun" makes me stop doubting whether I'm good enough, and cease pondering what could go wrong in my new relationship with a woman who loves me to bits already. Thank you Elizabeth Richardson. - Stew Shaw

I've always looked forward to reading your Confessions during the day. They've helped me to keep positive, strong and to stay true to myself. – Michelle Niese Hinshaw Steen

You make such a difference in this world. Love and light! – Patrick Carney

Thank you so much, Elizabeth. It's like you have picked me up and are moving with me, causing me to make a difference in my life at the exact right time that I need it. I am very grateful for your existence. Thank you, thank you, thank you. - Chupets Nano

Wow. You put Abraham in understandable English! What a blessing! – Joni Blumstein

I always look forward to reading your words. They make me, reconstruct me, shape me, re arrange me. They make me a better person! Thank you so much. – Jo-anne Mmela

The world needs your Confessions. – Dimple Pandey

Get The Most Out of This Book

This is Elizabeth.
Elizabeth is experienced.
She's done lots of Personal Development in an attempt to get results … and she's found that setting goals can often cloud the beauty of the present moment.
Be like Elizabeth.
Know the benefit of starting where you'd like to end up … and choose the experience you really want to have right now.

DAY 1: Living Happily Ever After … ☺

500 CONFESSIONS

(BOOK 2)

Progressive insights to boost CONFIDENCE gain CLARITY and radiate CHARISMA.

CONFESSION #501 …

I DECIDE I WANT SOMETHING … then get out of the way!

CONFESSION #502 ...

IT ALL BEGINS TODAY

More fun, more laughter, more joy, more light-heartedness, more delight, more intimacy, more deliciousness, more pleasure, more excitement, more touching, more loving, more ecstasy, more bliss ... with a little bit of drama thrown in for variety ... ☺

CONFESSION #503 ...

I'M BEING ASSISTED

If you don't think the Universe is conspiring to assist us all, then you forgot to watch the sun come up, without anyone needing to pay for it, making a business plan to get it, setting an intention about it, consciously asking for it, praying over it or begging for it.

Nature always adapts, bodies heal, lives transform, people help each other - heck, if you smiled at someone today, in that very moment, YOU assisted the world more than you probably give yourself credit for.

CONFESSION #504 …

I'M DELUSIONAL

I think life is always working out perfectly for me … ☺

CONFESSION #505 …

I'VE HAD HELP

The quality, ease and luxury of my life far exceeds anything I could have ever achieved alone.

For every time I didn't know how I'd pay the bills, for every bout of depression that caused me to refocus, for every business idea that failed, for every relationship that made me reach for something better, for every person who gave me grief - I thank you!

You made me resourceful, you made me grow, you made me stronger, you made me take better care of myself, you made me want to live a richer life, you made me learn how to really love, you made me find something far more sustainable and fulfilling, than winning the lottery could ever do.

You propelled me so much quicker, to where I was heading in the first place.

CONFESSION #506 …

I'M FAST

The quickest way to get to where I really want to be is, to change how I feel about where I am right now!

CONFESSION #507 …

I CAN CHANGE MY LIFE IN ABOUT 10 MINUTES

I might not be with my wonderful man right at this moment, but in 10 minutes I can open myself completely to remembering the deepest connection, unconditional support and Divine Joy he brings to my life.

I might not have the most streamlined body at the moment, but in 10 minutes I can list heaps of things I adore about the way it is right now.

I might not have all the luxurious assets I want just yet, but in 10 minutes I can vividly imagine how fabulous I'll feel when each one arrives.

In only 10 minutes my entire life can improve, without anything else changing at all. That's power, that's creation, that's REAL MAGIC!

CONFESSION #508 …

I'M IN CONTROL

I may not be able to change what's happening around me, but I definitely can control what I decide to focus on, I certainly do control how I choose to feel about it and I most powerfully intend to control how I will or won't respond to it.

THINGS I CAN CONTROL

- My ability to choose a better thought
- My freedom to change direction
- My decision to be fully aware in this moment
- My present attitude
- My current opinion
- My repetitive beliefs
- My direct focus
- My intention to feel good
- My choice to give and receive

THINGS I CAN INFLUENCE

- My alignment
- My energy level
- My weight
- My health
- My mood
- My vibe
- My level of charisma
- My inner spark
- My friends
- My bank manager
- My quality of life, just as it is.

CONFESSION #509 …

I LOVE MYSELF

I once thought that being liked was important. Now I know that *Loving Myself* is paramount!

CONFESSION #510 …

I FEEL SUCCESSFUL

I'm still alive ... lol

CONFESSION #511 ...

THERE IS ALWAYS HOPE

Every situation can be improved by:

- CHANGING A THOUGHT from despair to hope.
- CHANGING WORDS from "I don't know what to do" to "I'd like to know what to do".
- CHANGING FOCUS from discussing the problems to discovering solutions.
- CHANGING ATTITUDES from "life is hard" to "life presents endless opportunities".
- CHANGING BELIEFS from "it's impossible" to "you never know what might happen".
- CHANGING PHYSICAL POSITION from sitting to standing, inaction to action, clenched muscles to a more relaxed state, breathing shallow to breathing deeper.
- CHANGING A CHOICE from one of giving up an addiction to one of taking on better health.
- CHANGING LOCATION from being close to what's stimulating discomfort to closer to what stimulates peace.

The only way I can really help someone else is not by telling them what they should do, but by influencing through living my life as an example and allowing them the space to discover their own truth.

"Words Instruct - Demonstration Influences Experience Teaches."

CONFESSION #512 …

I DON'T HAVE A WORRY IN THE WORLD

I gave up watching the news years ago!

CONFESSION #513 …

I'M NEVER BORED

I've got a clitoris ... ☺

CONFESSION #514 …

I DON'T CARE WHAT YOU THINK OF ME!

If I cared what you might think of me, I wouldn't have a personality at all, I'd be a clone. I'd never have any fun, be a success, find fascinating things to be passionate about, get laid or fall in love.

It's not my job to conform to your standards so you can feel secure, so you can find peace, so you can be happy. It is each individual's task to find comfort, stillness and joy in the essence of their own soul.

Each time we ask someone to be different to who they really are, we drag them away from expressing their own desires, living their truth, following their calling and forging the most important life of all - their own!

CONFESSION #515 …

IT'S GOOD THAT I'M NOT PERFECT

If I was perfect you wouldn't grow. You'd become dependent on me being there forever and forget the incredible feeling of success you have … when you reach for something you want and get there, all by yourself.

If I was perfect you wouldn't be truly happy. You'd keep expecting me to be your entertainer, your mind reader, your rescuer, your mother, and never discover how brilliant you really are … when you need to step up and find happiness no matter where you are, no matter who you're with and no matter what's going on around you.

If I was perfect you wouldn't know your own power. You'd keep expecting me to be the catalyst for your alignment and never get to experience the peace, the security and the immense appreciation you feel … when you realize you truly are the creator of your own life.

If I was perfect you wouldn't become a leader. You'd keep putting me on a pedestal and try to knock me off instead of finding good reasons to lead the way yourself … when you are faced with something so big that it requires you to lift yourself up and carry others along with you.

If I was perfect you wouldn't learn how to love fully. You'd keep believing that love is about the worthiness of others instead of the incredible qualities you need to find deep inside yourself … when you have no other choice but to allow everything to be just as it is, or deny the amazing person you know you're really capable of being.

CONFESSION #516 …

I OFTEN DO THINGS THAT OTHERS WOULD DISAPPROVE OF

- but I don't make a big thing out of it,

- I don't make someone else wrong because of it,

- I don't get other people to agree with me before I do it,

- I don't get involved in conversations about the possible consequences of it and

- I don't FIGHT to have it.

Fighting for my rights keep the very things I don't want active. Integrity is a personal journey, and one I choose to take quietly and peacefully as often as possible.

CONFESSION #517 …

RELATIONSHIPS ARE GOOD FOR ME

I AM ALREADY HAPPY … but choosing someone to share life with helps me find joy, meaning and purpose so much quicker.

I AM ALREADY WISE … but being in a relationship provides greater opportunities to open my heart and mind even wider.

I AM ALREADY LOVED … but the simple things we do with each other expands my understanding of intimacy even more.

I AM ALREADY SPECIAL … but the way he treats me lets me know I'm the most precious jewel in the world to him.

I AM ALREADY WHOLE … but when our bodies are entwined or his hand is holding mine, it makes me feel even more complete.

I AM ALREADY BLESSED … but deciding to focus on only uplifting things about each other blesses both of us beyond description.

I AM ALREADY AT PEACE … but when we are together, it seems as if the soft essence of God is wrapping around us all and enhances my experience of life in greater degrees than I thought possible.

CONFESSION #518 ...

I QUIT

I quit struggling.
I quit doubting.
I quit second guessing my decisions.
I quit finding fault.
I quit trying so hard.
I quit being judgmental.
I quit expecting myself to be so perfect.

THEN I CHOOSE WHAT I PREFER TO HAVE INSTEAD

I choose to let it be easy.
I choose to have faith.
I choose to trust my decisions.
I choose to find positives.
I choose to follow joy, bliss, fun and pleasure.
I choose to love my mess.
I choose to see the funny side.
I choose to embrace my silliness.
I choose to be mostly happy and when I can't be happy, I choose ecstasy, exhilaration, appreciation and elation instead ... ☺

CONFESSION #519 ...

I'VE CHANGED FOR THE BETTER

BUSINESS WAS: How can I generate the most income? BUSINESS IS: How can I have the most fun?

A RELATIONSHIP WAS: How can I get my needs met? A RELATIONSHIP IS: How can I give, more of me?

FRIENDSHIP WAS: It's all about who I'm with! FRIENDSHIP IS: So much more about "Who I'm Being" no matter who I'm with!

A COMMITMENT WAS: A vow I needed from another so I could feel safe. A COMMITMENT IS: A vow I make with myself to regularly re-connect with my own Inner Security, no matter what the other is up to.

MONEY WAS: Something I thought I needed so that I could have everything I want.

MONEY IS: Something that just breathes in and out naturally, as a result of choosing to feel exactly how I want.

CREDIBILITY WAS: Something I thought I needed to earn so I could be valued by others. CREDIBILITY IS: Something I declare privately I AM, so I value myself first.

BEING ATTRACTIVE WAS: Achieving an outward appearance that would make me feel happy. BEING ATTRACTIVE IS: Aligning with a happy Inner Radiance, that just makes me shine.

BEING A SUCCESS ONCE MEANT: Proving to others how incredible I am. BEING A SUCCESS REALLY MEANS: Knowing so profoundly that "I Am Enough!"

BEING LOVED WAS: Something I defined by how others were treating me. BEING LOVED IS: Something that just comes easily, when I treat myself well first.

MY MISSION WAS: To bring light to a dark world so I could prove my life had great value. MY MISSION NOW IS: To thrive, to have fun, to find blessings, to feel joy! "I'm Not Here to Bring Light To The World, I'm Here To BE The Light!"

MY JOB AS A PARENT WAS: Warning my kids about problems they might face. MY JOB AS A PARENT REALLY IS: Encouraging them to listen to their own Inner Guidance, knowing they'll find their own way much easier, if I get out of it.

CONNECTION WAS: Something I needed to have with another so I could feel grounded and whole. CONNECTION IS: Feeling a "Sense of Oneness" with everything without needing to change anyone or anything else at all.

CONFESSION #520 …

I DON'T PAY MUCH ATTENTION TO WHERE YOU'RE AT

If I thought twice about how you're feeling, I'd be living my life affected profoundly by your moods. When you're feeling good, I'd feel good, and when you're feeling bad, I'd feel rotten. Nothing you do can affect me negatively for very long, unless I keep giving it my attention, keep complaining about it, keep on making you "wrong" for doing it and foolishly forget that I have my own life to live

CONFESSION #521 ...

LIFE IS AS EASY AS I MAKE IT

It's just as easy to "decide that good things are happening" as it is to think things are bad. It's just as easy to "create wealth" as it is to make money. And the difference depends entirely, on what I intend to give my attention to from this moment on!

- AM I trying to make a living or create a life?

- AM I trying to make do or create anew?

- AM I trying to make ends meet or create a dream?

- AM I trying to make something happen or create more fun?

- AM I trying to motivate myself to action or create inspired responses?

- AM I trying to work harder or create a life of ease?

- AM I trying to get rid of something I've already got or create reasons to appreciate what I already have?

- AM I trying to change something on the outside or create a more harmonious Inner World?

- AM I trying to impress someone else or create a closer alignment with Myself?

- AM I trying to fix the past or create an improved tomorrow?

- AM I trying to live up to old expectations or create a brand new story?

"The difference you *FEEL* by changing your attitude, will astound you."

CONFESSION #522 ...

I LOVE MEN

This is Elizabeth.
Elizabeth is wise.
She doesn't claim to be a new age conscious woman,
nor does she make innuendos about wanting an awakened man.
Elizabeth knows there are lots of fun things she can do to a man who is asleep ... ☺
Be like Elizabeth.
Play with Life.

CONFESSION #523 …

MY SOUL IS CALLING

I've imagined you for an eternity, from deep inside my mind. I have watched you soundly sleeping with your heart right next to mine. I walked across the water your hungry soul to seek, as if by chance I'd see you there, my body craving for us to meet.

But I wanted you to find me; it was something I did ask. My searching was so frustrating and not a woman's task. I thank God you heard me calling bringing sunshine to my eyes, and paved the way for us to meet with such a sweet surprise.

Your voice so recognizable I knew without a doubt, and we talked as if forever, had known us inside out. Now that I can feel you, so intimately by my side, I want to savor these precious moments anticipation cannot hide.

There have been one thousand angels who've conspired to draw us near. They felt the longing of my soul and knew the crying of my tears.

Your lips were made to catch them, my pining heart to calm, and your arms were made to hold me and protect me from all harm.

You've asked, what have I done to you? I called you from afar. The heavens caused the earth to move the sun the moon and stars. For us to be reunited, the time has finally come, and when we look into each other's eyes, we'll remember the feeling, of coming home.

CONFESSION #524 …

I LOVE MYSELF SO MUCH

… that I won't speak badly about someone else simply because it makes ME feel bad. I refuse to see them in a negative light because it takes my emotions into a downward spin. Instead I'll find something interesting, something unique or something funny to say about them and send my emotions soaring upwards again.

I LOVE MYSELF SO MUCH

… that I won't allow myself to feel worse by focusing on how someone else is behaving when they're disconnected from who they really are. I can't change what they've done in the past by talking about it, I can't change what they're doing now by making it wrong and I certainly can't change what they're about to do in the future by condemning them. But I can change how I'm feeling by giving them space and time, and by trusting they're finding their own way too, just as I am finding mine.

I LOVE MYSELF SO MUCH

… that I get over what other people are doing with their lives and get on with being a good example with mine.

I LOVE MYSELF SO MUCH

… that no matter what someone else has done, no matter if they have very few redeeming qualities, no matter if they seem like the worst person in the world, I'll find just ONE thing good about them and expand on that.

I LOVE MYSELF SO MUCH

… that I only speak well of myself and others. In the moment I tell someone something negative, I am projecting separation through a judgment from my mind. In the moment I tell someone something positive, I am reflecting wholeness and the wisdom of the Divine.

CONFESSION #525 …

I KNOW WHO I AM AND WHAT I WANT FOR MY LIFE

I KNOW THAT I'M EXACTLY WHERE I NEED TO BE … and that it's the perfect place from which to choose another new adventure or continue the one I'm already enjoying.

I AM THOUGHTFUL … of what I allow to soak into my mind. I reach for the most loving thoughts I can find. I am careful of the words that escape from my lips and delight in spreading good news wherever I go.

I AM AWARE … that the entire Universe is always bringing me cooperative people, events and circumstances that show me the most active thoughts vibrating through my energy field, even though the deeper meaning may not be apparent at the time.

I THRIVE ON BEING INVOLVED IN UPLIFTING CONVERSATIONS … that increase life force, not draw energy away from it.

I UNCONDITIONALLY ACCEPT … all people, all lifestyles, all choices, all religions, all beliefs and especially my own uniquely individual nature and affirm that each one of us is doing the best we know how in any given moment.

I UNDERSTAND … that what I give my attention to expands, and that all emotions, all thoughts, all words, all deeds, all natural disasters, all world events are part of the whole and know that each situation gives me the perfect opportunity to decide what I prefer to focus on, find solutions for, make bigger or create more of.

I ALIGN MY LIFE … with love, with happiness, with clarity, with joy, with bliss, with freedom, with fun, with passion, with peace (with any positive emotion) and with appreciation for "All That Is". In doing this, I effortlessly add even more value to the world … by just being myself.

I USE MY MIND INTENTIONALLY … to focus on the good in myself, the best qualities in others and the greatest possible benefit in every situation.

I FIND RELIEF IN THE BEST WAY I CAN … with no judgment about what is right or wrong, better or worse, good or bad and understand that it is guilt which keeps people stuck in a never-ending loop of pain, anger, suffering and addiction. I choose to let go of guilt forever, and enjoy my fucking life!

I ACKNOWLEDGE THAT THE SIMPLE THINGS IN LIFE ARE PROFOUNDLY VALUABLE … the smell of freshly baked bread, the taste of the finest quality fudge, the sound of children laughing, the sight of two lovers connecting, the feeling of spiritual communion inside my own heart and mind … and allow plenty of space to enjoy all the delightful luxuries that nurture my material desires as well.

I DO WHATEVER FEELS RIGHT IN THE MOMENT … and no longer need other people's approval, permission, validation, endorsement, acceptance or understanding for anything at all. I've stopped explaining or justifying who I am, what I'm doing and where I'm at and just quietly, gracefully and happily live the life that's right for me.

I GO TO SLEEP PEACEFULLY … imagining happy things, uplifting things, pleasant things, beautiful things and wake up feeling refreshed with a smile of deep gratitude simply for the gift of enjoying yet another day on this amazing planet.

I TRUST MY OWN INNER GUIDANCE … to lead me towards the light, to provide relief, to help me feel better, to answer my questions, to solve my problems, to infuse me with passion, to show me real Love and to provide infinite options to choose from, whenever I'm inspired to do so.

I THANKFULLY ACCEPT AND RECEIVE SUPPORT FROM SOURCE … on all levels, physical, emotional, mental, financial and spiritual; without having to work hard, without needing to strive, without defining an action plan, without forcing an outcome. I simply follow the calling of my own Inner Guidance, appreciate how much I've already been given and allow even more good things to flow naturally into my life.

I ALLOW SPACE FOR YOU TO BE WHO YOU ARE … and encourage you to follow your own Inner Knowing, to feel in your body if something is nourishing, to know in your heart if something is good, to sense in your soul if something is right; NOT to listen to what I or others might think is appropriate … and to always remember that YOU are the most powerful director of your own life too.

"I direct my magnificent life and so do you!"

CONFESSION #526 …

I'M MAKING A WISH

But not for more money, not for another beautiful home, not for improved conditions, not for better fitness, not for a magnificent lover ... (ok ok the magnificent lover might be coming today) … but seriously, I'm making a wish to feel how I imagine I'll feel, as each of those wonderful things fall neatly, effortlessly and comfortably into place, right where they belong.

"I wish … TO FEEL GOOD RIGHT NOW!"

CONFESSION #527 …

I'M CREATING QUALITY MOMENTS

I don't care if a relationship lasts a long time, I just do whatever I can to make it "a good time" every time we are together.

I don't care if I live a long time, I just want to live a useful life, a full life, a happy life and a life filled with expansion, openness, integrity, freedom, focus, joy and love.

CONFESSION #528 …

I DON'T CLAIM TO BE A MASTER OF ANYTHING

I prefer to be a mistress instead, tall black vinyl boots, red garter, tight laced bodice, long flowing hair, wicked smile … ☺

CONFESSION #529 …

I LOVE THIS UNIVERSE

I Love Money ... and I like how you keep showing me interesting, unique and different ways for money to flow.

I Love My Body ... and I adore how you keep my blood pumping, my heart beating, my cells regenerating, my hair growing, my eyes seeing, my muscles strengthening, my system thriving.

I Love Relationships ... and I really appreciate how you keep matching me with like-minded, funny, easy-going, gorgeous, happy, uplifting people.

I Love Intimacy ... and oh my goodness, I'm blown away by the intensely pleasurable sensations I get to experience in conscious communion with others.

I Love Animals ... and I'm incredibly happy to be blessed by their company, their beauty, their entertaining presence, their balancing energy, their unconditional acceptance.

I Love Food ... and wow, thank you for providing me with so much variety, so many textures, scintillating flavours, such deliciously enjoyable fuel.

I Love This Planet ... and I'm in awe with how you keep the sun rising, the rain falling, the plants growing, the soil replenishing, the rivers flowing and all of life evolving.

I Love Clarity ... and I'm thoroughly delighted to be gifted daily infusions of Energy, Creativity, Passion, Vision and Purpose.

I Love To Focus ... and I greatly appreciate how you keep guiding me to thoughts, ideas and actions, that are in harmony with my core Desires.

I Love Alignment ...and I really, really like how you keep bringing me evidence of how life works best, in comfortable, humorous and the most delightful ways.

Thank You. I Cherish You. I Love You.

CONFESSION #530 …

I TURN MYSELF ON

Feeling like a real woman, has little to do with how a man is behaving and everything to do with the way I nurture my body, tune in my mind and connect to my soul, The right guy just gets to exclusively experience the fullness of that Sexual Energy, if he's very, very good … ☺

SEXUAL energy IS SPIRITUAL energy. That's why most people, no matter what their beliefs, culture, race or religion, spontaneously call out to "God" in the throes of their deepest passion.

But there is sexual energy, stemming from negative emotion that SEEKS to satisfy itself. And there is sexual energy, stemming from positive emotions, that's INSPIRED to express its wholeness.

CONFESSION #531 …

I LOVE SEX

I love porn, I love orgasm and I love my body.

I have absolutely NO RULES about what's appropriate for me or anyone else. If something feels good, I do it again, and again, and again. I myself decide what's right for me; not the church, not my parents, not my family, not society and not even my mate need to approve, accept it or agree.

CONFESSION #532 …

I CONQUERED ADDICTIONS

When I wanted to change an old HABIT I don't have to learn how to say "no" to whatever I though the problem was, that just kept my attention on the issue. Instead, I keep saying "yes" to something new.

I'm saying yes to a new way of thinking
I'm saying yes to starting again
I'm saying yes to giving myself a break
I'm saying yes to lightening up a little
I'm saying yes to making peace with where I am
I'm saying yes to telling happier stories
I'm saying yes to doing things different
I'm saying yes to changing my posture
I'm saying yes to finding relief
I'm saying yes to moving my body
I'm saying yes to quietening my mind more often
I'm saying yes to taking more naps
I'm saying yes to looking forward
I'm saying yes to imagining positive outcomes
I'm saying yes to improved health
I'm saying yes to getting more massages
I'm saying yes to deciding where I want to go
I'm saying yes to waiting for inspiration
I'm saying yes to a higher quality of life

I'm saying yes to remembering the good times
I'm saying yes to talking about my success
I'm saying yes to having more fun
I'm saying yes to laughing out loud
I'm saying yes to freedom
I'm saying yes to turning myself on
I'm saying yes to knowing real pleasure
I'm saying yes to breathing even deeper
I'm saying yes to feeling so much better
I'm saying yes to opening my heart
I'm saying yes to being more focused
I'm saying yes to treating myself well
I'm saying yes to accepting how far I've come
I'm saying yes to liking who I am again
I'm saying yes to love

CONFESSION #533 …

I LOVE HAVING ALL AREAS OF MY LIFE HANDLED

MONEY … flows in and out, in and out like the air that I breathe. There's always more where that came from.

FREEDOM MEANS… Being free to choose my focus, my beliefs, my attitude, my responses, is perfectly natural for me.

WORK MEANS … Doing whatever I love to do. Security comes from living my dreams now, not working towards them later.

A COMMITMENT MEANS … Staying true to my-self.

LOVE MEANS … I'm selfish. I choose to love you, because loving feels so good.

RELATIONSHIP MEANS … When my relationship with my Inner-Being is aligned in love, all other relationships are easy. Some come, some go, some stay, some walk away, but love still remains.

LIFE MEANS ... Demonstrating my alignment as often as I can. Feeling good is the most important thing to me. Everything else is inspired from there.

PARENTING MEANS ... Allowing others the space to find their own alignment. Personal integrity is born from personal experience.

FRIENDSHIP MEANS ... I am my own best friend first and I appreciate the new ones, the long term ones and those still to be made.

OTHER PEOPLE ... What others are being, doing or creating is none of my business. I leave it to God to manage. That's a relief ... ☺

MY SELF ... Acknowledging who I've been, loving who I am, adoring who I'm becoming.

MY JOURNEY ... Accepting where I've been, appreciating where I am, celebrating where I'm going.

MY HEART ... It isn't breaking, it's expanding.

MY HOME ... I find beauty, peace, comfort and luxury no matter where I am in the world.

CONFESSION #534 …

I'M IMPRESSED BY PEOPLE WHO HAVE AN ABUNDANCE OF MONEY

And I'm even more impressed by people who have an abundance of happiness, satisfaction and fulfilment, whether they have lots of money or not.

CONFESSION #535 …

I CAN'T STOP IT

Good stuff keeps happening, whether I'm feeling perfectly aligned, in the zone, totally in tune or not.

CONFESSION #536 …

I TRUST MY INSTINCTS

I know when something seems a bit "off" and when it feels "right". I know when someone's telling the truth and when they're trying to say what they think I want to hear. I also know that when I'm feeling really good, how other people are behaving, doesn't affect me at all.

CONFESSION #537 …

I FOUND THE EASY WAY TO HAVE A HAPPIER DAY

Emphasize everything that feels good and minimize anything that doesn't. I talk incessantly about what makes my heart sing, I bask endlessly in the fullness of my own creativity, I amplify loudly my appreciation for the perfection of life, I dramatize boldly the stories of happy times and expand further on whatever inspires hope, comfort, peace, understanding, freedom, delight and joy.

CONFESSION #538 …

I TAKE GOOD CARE OF MYSELF

When I RESPECT Myself … I don't tolerate someone else's crap, I don't take what they're saying or doing personally, I don't even stay in the same room if it feels uncomfortable, and after a while, they show respect for me too (or they just disappear from my experience).

When I VALUE Myself … I expect to be treated well, paid well and appreciated well, and after a while, it just comes naturally.

When I LOVE Myself … I think thoughts that feel good, have conversations that feel good, go to places that feel good and hang around with people who feel good … and before long I notice, that the ones who really matter, cherished, respected and valued me anyway.

"The most important relationship is the one between My Source and My Self".

CONFESSION #539 …

I'VE BEEN ON A LOT OF DATES

I've dated a multi billionaire, a famous sportsman, a celebrity, a bankrupt, men who adored me, worshiped me, supported me and those who've stayed friends through thick and thin with me, but nothing opens me more than a man who stays true to himself, no matter how much he's in love with me!

CONFESSION #540 …

YOU CAN'T BREAK MY HEART

The only time I ever had a broken heart, was when I expected someone else to give me something, that I clearly wasn't giving myself.

CONFESSION #541 ...

I KEEP LOVE CLOSE

I SPEAK so lovingly about my ex that many people thought we were destined to get back together. But there was method in my madness!

I KNEW the loving conversations were really opening my heart even wider to a more expansive kind of love - maybe with him OR maybe with someone else.

CONFESSION #542 …

I'M UNDERSTANDING

Real understanding is when I understand that other people might not understand … ☺

- When I allow them to make their choices without trying to change them.

- When I simply accept they have their own valid reasons for doing what they do.

- When I can see that I'm usually doing the very thing that I have accused them of doing.

- When I can let them show me the dark side of their personality and still hold onto the precious knowing, of the innate Light inside their Soul.

CONFESSION #543 …

I HAVE ASSETS

- A financial asset is something that increases the amount of money in your pocket.

- An emotional asset makes you feel better than you did before.

- A mental asset adds positivity to your outlook.

- A spiritual asset aligns you with "Who You Really Are"; someone who already has all the assets they could ever need to expand their life experience and reach comfortably for the very next thing they desire.

CONFESSION #544 …

I HAVE BIG PLANS

I plan to be happy and follow my bliss. Yep, that's pretty much it! … ☺

CONFESSION #545 …

I CAN IMPROVE MY MOOD QUICKLY

By stopping to take a few deep breaths, quietening my mind in meditation, drinking freshly chilled water, concentrating on something I enjoy greatly, doing pelvic floor exercises, moving my body in a sensual way, but most easily, by declaring whatever is bothering me, irrelevant!

CONFESSION #546 …

I ADORE WHO I AM

To start loving myself fully, I had to stop criticizing myself completely.

CONFESSION #547 ...

I DO THINGS THAT PLEASE ME

This is Elizabeth.

Elizabeth is on a diet.

While she might no longer

enjoy eating candy,

she still gets great pleasure ...

from looking at it ... ☺

CONFESSION #548 …

I'M SUFFERING

From chronic joy, explosive laughter, terminal hopefulness, intermittent ecstasy, semi-permanent bliss, overwhelming love, exaggerated passion, obsessive optimism and annoyingly persistent happiness … beware, it might be catching!

CONFESSION #549 …

I'M ENJOYING A SPIRITUAL RELATIONSHIP

The goal isn't to find a mate with particular qualities. The task is to live your life predominantly in the emotional state of your choice, and naturally, vibrationally and Divinely draw to you those people, places and opportunities to match that. It shouldn't be difficult. It's meant to be joyful, exciting and fun.

In The Power Of Now, Eckhart Tolle talks about using relationships as a "Spiritual Practice"; an opportunity to raise yourself above the common judgement of the other persons actions as being either loving or unloving. Experiencing the pain but NOT attaching thought, explanation or reasons to it, thus allowing it to pass naturally.

This has personally been one of the most empowering re-frames of my life. My relationship is my spiritual practice and my mate doesn't even need to be present, to know about it, to participate OR to be real.

CONFESSION #550 ...

I HAVE FUN WHEREVER I GO

This is Elizabeth.

Elizabeth is on Facebook.

Relationship Status: imaginary ... 😜

CONFESSION #551 …

I VALUE PROSPERITY AND ABUNDANCE

MENTAL WEALTH – Your accumulation of knowledge, research, planning, skills, experience etc. that can be utilized at any given moment and put into action.

PHYSICAL WELL-BEING – The fitness, health, respect and care of your body that largely determines mental acuity and how much you are able to actively do towards creating wealth for yourself and others now, and into the future.

FINANCIAL RESOURCEFULNESS – Ready access to money and assets that generate an exchange of energy, goods, services or property.

RELATIONAL AFFINITY – The richness of your relationships with other people, staff, family, business associates, financiers etc. These define your ease of access to physical resources, financial assistance, mental upliftment and emotional support.

EMOTIONAL INTEGRITY – The regular attunement to positive, life-giving emotions which are usually practiced in daily rituals like meditation, exercise, dance, yoga, stillness, music, creative pursuits, journalling and any activity that connects you more fully to your Source Of Power, Infinite Intelligence and Aligned Inspiration.

INTENTIONAL FUTURE – Are you taking responsibility for your own health, happiness and prosperity now and into the future or are you relying on God, the government or someone else to provide for you?

VIBRATIONAL ABUNDANCE – The ability to allow the natural flow of goodwill from The Universe. This can be measured by the underlying thoughts, beliefs and attitudes that contribute to how you feel, most often evident in your current physical manifestations, how much energy you have in each moment and your conversations about what's "probable" for the future.

ATTITUDINAL RICHNESS – How do you feel about wealthy people, powerful individuals, governments, multinational companies, political leaders, well paid actors/sports stars,

CEO'S etc.? Do you assume they are ripping people off, abusing their own power, rorting the system, too rich to care about others? Do you rally against them, speak badly about them, eagerly pass on negative gossip and voice your opinion publicly? OR do you accept, support, celebrate them and understand that they are human beings doing the best they know how too?

SPIRITUAL PROSPERITY – A balance of all of the above along with having a sense of meaning, clarity, Divine Connection, purpose, worthiness, value and mission in life. Without this feeling, people suicide on a daily basis … what use is money then?

CONFESSION #552 …

I HAVE A SELECTIVE MEMORY

I remember the things that bring me joy, the feelings that still my mind, the words that brighten my day, the beauty that makes me smile, the peace that warms my soul and the love that makes my heart feel whole.

You know that disagreement we had yesterday? I can't even remember what it was about. My selective memory sorted that all out!

CONFESSION #553 …

I MAKE POWERFUL DECISIONS

The immense power of any decision is when I stay aligned with it; not to entertain doubt, not to speak of failure, not to question my worthiness, not to wonder how it could possibly happen; but to know that all Universal Forces join with me in creating momentum forward, no matter how big or small this thing I've asked for is.

"I never question my decisions. I just stay faithful to them."

CONFESSION #554 …

MY TEN COMMANDMENTS

Simple strategies to help me live a more fulfilled life:

1. Breathe deeper (always helpful, unless I'm underwater).

2. Take notice of what I'm thinking and make sure it's about things I DO want, not about what I don't.

3. Only get involved in conversations that are uplifting.

4. Write down the positive aspects of every situation that's causing me discomfort.

5. Spend as much time as possible appreciating everything I've already been given and being thankful for what's still to come.

6. Make sure my beliefs line up with what I want for my life.

7. Allow other people the space to grow, to live their own lives and to not become dependent on me for anything.

8. Give to myself first. When I fill myself up, the overflow naturally showers others.

9. Be authentic. Follow my bliss. Live the life that's right for me, in tune with my own integrity.

10. Do whatever it takes to align myself with my Inner-Being/ God/ Love and then allow all thoughts, words and actions be inspired from that place of deeper knowing.

CONFESSION #555 …

I CAN CHANGE WHAT I'M ATTRACTING

When I stop looking at what others are "Doing" and start "Being" the incredible person I know is really me, in the moment I stop complaining and behave like the leader I was really born to be.

When I cease the negative gossip but share news that brightens up the day, as I STOP in the throes of telling the same old story yet stay silent, until I've found the right words to describe it in a more uplifting way!

When I no longer compare myself to others and just be Who I Want To Be, as soon as I stop trying to achieve a particular result and simply let MORE good things flow to me.

Whenever I stop blaming the government and keep affirming, times are tough, realizing that when I've needed it, there's always been enough.

At the times I cease the endless pushing and start learning to allow, when I no longer declare, "I deserve something better" and just trust it's on its way to me right now!

When I remember that once I've asked, something even better will often come. As I take a deeper breath and have faith, that what I want, is already Divinely done!

CONFESSION #556 …

I AM POWERFUL

I knew I'd claimed my own power, when I stopped asking others to approve, to endorse or to agree with me about anything.

CONFESSION #557 …

NOTHING CAN STOP ME

- What I CAN do, is only limited by my desire to do it.
- My budget is only limited by my creativity.
- My mood is only limited by what I'm giving the most attention to.
- The quality of my life is only limited by my story about it.
- Going out on a date, is only limited by my willingness to say "yes".
- The closeness of my relationship is only limited by my attitude towards my mate.
- What I can have, is only limited by what I'll allow myself to believe.
- Where I can go, is only limited by my imagination.
- What is possible to make real … has no limits at all.

CONFESSION #558 …

I TRUST

I trust my feelings - period! If something feels "off" I know it. If something feels ordinary, I don't bother with it. If something feels good, I go for it. What other people are doing becomes irrelevant. The quality of my life is based on how well I listen to my own guidance, not on evaluating what someone else is doing with theirs.

CONFESSION #559 ...

I SPEAK MINDFULLY

This is Elizabeth.
Elizabeth is wise.
She knows that when she complains about other people being negative, she is actually being negative about them being negative.
Elizabeth realizes that when she criticizes the President or anyone else, she's really saying more about herself than she could possibly say about them.
Be wise like Elizabeth
Shut the duck up! ... ☺

CONFESSION #560 …

I DON'T FIGHT FOR WHAT I WANT

I never need to fight for anything. I just stopped affirming that someone else could prevent me from having it.

CONFESSION #561 …

I'M AT HOME IN NATURE

THE SUN ... soothes my body.
THE WIND ... freshens my mind.
THE STARS ... excites my imagination.
THE MOON ... liberates my emotions.
THE EARTH ... grounds my energy.
THE GRASS ... caresses my skin.
THE TREES ... stimulate my senses.
THE WATER ... washes away my worries.
THE SAND … softens my fall.
THE SUNRISE ... opens my heart.

CONFESSION #562 …

I HAVE AN AMAZING LIFE

Not because I was given some special gift, not because I have everything I could possible need, not because I was born lucky and not because of good karma. I choose how I want to experience life each day, with as much peace, bliss, joy, elation and ecstasy as I can possibly allow.

CONFESSION #563 …

I DON'T FACE REALITY

Reality is something I can consciously create moment by moment with a simple intention to follow my bliss, to choose what feels better, to see things in a different light, to find the benefits, to acknowledge the blessings, to sense good things coming, to imagine the possibilities, to expect improvement and to notice natural abundance. Creating realities is what allows miracles, restores wellness, reaffirms loving feelings and changes the world in the most profound ways.

One uplifted person who regularly finds Inner Alignment, holds more influence than millions who are looking outside themselves for answers.

"You don't change things by looking at WHAT IS. You change things by looking towards WHAT YOU WANT TO SEE instead."

CONFESSION #564 …

I FACE TOWARDS THE SOLUTION

If I have a problem, I trust the solution is on its way. If I have a question, I know I'll find the answer in due course. If I'm feeling confused, I know that clarity is just around the corner. If I think my life is in a mess, I decide to believe I'm getting closer and closer, towards the life I've been really dreaming of living. And so it is.

*"On the opposite side of the darkest problem is the most *BRILLIANT SOLUTION*"*
I'm lining up with that!

CONFESSION #565 …

I'M RESPECTED

Not because I gave other people what they wanted, but because I stayed true to "What I Wanted" … ☺

CONFESSION #566 ...

I'M LOVED

Not because I gave so much to other people that they wanted to give me something in return, but because I treated "Myself" so well and showed them how it's done!

CONFESSION #567 …

I LIVE REALLY WELL

Not because I work hard for a living, but because I look for as much ease, fun, delight, excitement and pleasure as I can possibly handle and the enjoyment alone, far surpasses anything that money can buy.

CONFESSION #568 …

I AM AT PEACE

Not because my life is any better than yours, not because I fought hard to get it and not because I was born lucky. I'm at peace because no matter who I'm with, where I am or what's going on in the world, I only focus my attention on things that make me feel good.

CONFESSION #569 …

I'M RICH

Not because I have more stuff than other people, but because I chose to be happy whether I had the stuff or not.

CONFESSION #570 ...

I PLAY ALL DAY

I don't work hard to get something I want,
I play my way there ... ☺

CONFESSION #571 …

THE MOST REWARDING THING I'VE EVER DONE

When I decided to be kind to someone even though they weren't being kind to me, when I allowed someone their freedom even though they tried to take away mine, when I kept on loving even though I thought my heart was breaking, when I gave more of what I had to offer even though I'd already given enough.

"In that moment I discovered, I AM ENOUGH."

CONFESSION #572 …

I USE MY ASSETS TO MY ADVANTAGE

This is Elizabeth.
Elizabeth is a transforming.
She once thought she needed to make HUGE changes to improve her life.
But she found that changing the little everyday things is what makes the biggest difference.
So now, rather than looking at her flaws in the mirror, she takes the time to write down the positive attributes she likes instead.

Great breasts - really happy with those … lol

CONFESSION #573 …

I HOPE I NEVER GET SERIOUS

Serious never accomplished anything worthwhile. It's time to GET HAPPY!

Happy with who you've become, happy with what you have achieved, happy with the life you are living, happy with the new adventure you're about to embark on. Make peace with where you are then let your naturally vivacious, uplifting, fun-loving nature, guide you home.

CONFESSION #574 …

I EXPECT EVERYTHING TO GO WELL

… and it does.

I imagine things are just the way I want them, and it makes me feel fabulous. I talk as if I already have everything I could possibly desire, and even more wonderful things come along that set my world on fire. I believe that life is meant to be easy and fun and love-filled and exiting and absolutely anything I want it to be, and so it is.

CONFESSION #575 …

I'VE HAD A *BREAKTHROUGH*

I finally stopped doing the little resistant things I once thought were too insignificant to matter … ☺

CONFESSION #576 …

I'M TRUE TO MYSELF

When I am being true to myself, I don't care what others think, I don't look to them for feedback, I don't need them to approve of me. I care MORE about how I feel! I listen closely to my own Inner Guidance and sense intrinsically the immense value that my demonstration offers all.

CONFESSION #577 …

I LAUGH AT MYSELF

This is Elizabeth.
Elizabeth hasn't been on a date in a while.
She doesn't have a long list of criteria
that a man should live up to.
She's just happy if he is human and
breathing.

DON'T be like Elizabeth.
Elizabeth is desperate … lol

CONFESSION #578 …

WHEN I WANTED A HAPPIER LIFE

I didn't complain about it. I just focused more and more on the things that made me happy and the unpleasant elements drifted away.

CONFESSION #579 …

WHEN I WANTED A HAPPIER RELATIONSHIP

I didn't tell anyone else about how bad it was, I just concentrated on the parts that made me feel comforted and the annoying aspects drifted away.

(lol … the annoying mate drifted away too and made space for a beautiful, loving warm, intimate and aligned relationship instead).

CONFESSION #580 ...

I LEFT A RELATIONSHIP BEHIND

But not because I was angry, not because he was wrong, not because something bad happened and not because I thought I should. It happened spontaneously when I was feeling really good, nothing was planned, the right words were inspired, it was over and done and I felt complete.

CONFESSION #581 …

I NEVER ASK PEOPLE TO TELL ME THEIR TROUBLES

My real job is to find out what sets their soul on fire.

CONFESSION #582 …

I'M GOOD

But life isn't about how good I am. It's about Who I Am. And I'm someone who thrives at all times, I'm someone who always gives everything I want to give without needing anything in return, I'm someone who finds joy in even the most mundane things, I'm someone who uplifts, I'm someone who follows my own heart, I'm someone who stays true to what's right for me, I'm someone who seeks to reveal the blessing in every situation and I'm someone who knows implicitly the goodness inside every human soul.

- I LIVE with deep understanding.
- I SPEAK with sound clarity.
- I WRITE with a distinct attitude.
- I SING with unique harmony.
- I LOVE with pure innocence.
- I LAUGH with sheer abandon.
- I BE with raw honesty.
- I ALIGN with my own Soul.

CONFESSION #583 …

SOMETIMES I'M BAD,

But, I was born to be happy, not to behave. I was born to follow my dreams, not to chase the visions of others. I was born to love with all of my heart, not to be afraid that my heart might break. I was born to enjoy this moment, to feel its passion, to play, to laugh and to follow my inspiration. I was born to live fully, to love unconditionally, to grow gracefully, to contribute quietly, to laugh heartily and to build people up. I was born to live in harmony with my Higher Self and all of life. I was born to be free, and I was born to be ME!

CONFESSION #584 ...

THERE ARE THINGS I JUST WON'T DO

- If a thought doesn't feel good ... then I won't think it!

- If a conversation doesn't sound uplifting ... then I won't get involved in it!

- If a news story doesn't make me happy ... then I won't watch it!

- If a belief limits my potential ... then I stop repeating it!

Whatever I focus on gets bigger, so I choose to focus on things that make me feel the way I want to feel instead.

CONFESSION #585 …

I AM RESPONSIBLE FOR MY RESPONSES

Your behaviour is not my responsibility, but my response to it is.

I don't try to remove negative things from my life, I keep enjoying the best parts and let go of the strife. I never need to push people away, I just open my doors wide, to those who really want to stay. I don't bother to declare how other people should be, I decided it was more important, to just "BE HAPPY BEING ME".

CONFESSION #586 …

WHO I AM … is enough!

CONFESSION #587 …

HEAVEN KNOWS

I might not know how things are going to work out, but God does! Relax. There's far more to life than meets the eye.

CONFESSION #588 ...

I'M HAPPY

- When I'm happy I feel connected.

- When I'm happy I am successful.

- When I'm happy I don't have a worry in the world.

- When I'm happy everything works perfectly.

- When I'm happy anything seems possible.

- When I'm happy everyone looks even more beautiful.

- When I'm happy I remember how Loved I really am.

CONFESSION #589 …

I'M UNREAL

This is Elizabeth.
Elizabeth is wise.
It's morning here in Australia
and Elizabeth wouldn't dream of claiming
to be an awakened woman at all.
Heck, she's not even
a real woman … ☺

CONFESSION #590 …

I MEDITATE REGULARLY

When things didn't seem like they would turn out, I relaxed a little more, changed my point of view, meditated on my navel, took time out alone, asked silently for help, felt my spirits raise, found a glimmer of hope and then watched with amusement, as it turned out even better.

CONFESSION #591 …

I HAVE HIGH STANDARDS

I wouldn't share a story about something just because it's true. I tell a story because it makes me feel good to spread it around.

Most people have opinions about how others should behave. I just have high standards, for how I intend to feel, no matter how they're behaving!

I have very high standards for a relationship too. But the standards I set are for MY behaviour, not for my mate. I intend to flow as much love and appreciation towards him as I can, not because he deserves it, not because I feel obligated, not because I'm supposed to, not even because I made a promise, but because it feels like heaven to flow Divine Loving Energy from my inside, out.

CONFESSION #592 …

I'VE CHANGED MY PERSPECTIVE

Whatever I thought was stopping me from having what I want, is actually helping me to define it more clearly. Whatever seemed to be causing concern is really a blessing in disguise. What felt like the hardest relationship of my life has just paved the perfect path for me to attract the BEST one for all eternity. What seemed like uncomfortable turmoil has transformed into the most peaceful certainty about Who I Am, What I Want and Where I Intend to Take My Life.

CONFESSION #593 …

I'M EXCITED ABOUT LIFE

If something doesn't turn out how I thought it might, I know that something even better is right around the corner.

"The only difference between despair and hope, is the story I tell myself."

CONFESSION #594 …

I DIRECT THE COURSE OF MY LIFE

By noticing what doesn't feel right and lining up faithfully and whole heartedly, with what does.

CONFESSION #595 ...

I GET LOTS OF PRACTICE

This is Elizabeth.
Elizabeth has standards.
She doesn't believe in going out with any guy just to pass the time!
But hang on, she's also realized
it might be a good idea
to get some practice at dating again.

Be wise like Elizabeth.
Just get another cat ... ☺

CONFESSION #596 …

I'VE FOUND INCREDIBLE POWER

1. By giving love without expecting anything in return.

2. By meeting my own needs without expecting it to come in any particular way.

3. By finding that peaceful place inside without expecting other people or situations to change at all.

CONFESSION #597 …

I'VE CREATED MY IDEAL MATE

THIS MAN
Knows what he has and cherishes it
Knows what he wants, and goes for it
Takes good care of himself on all levels
Is aligned with his source and lives with integrity
In his heart he is committed
In his mind he is focused
In his work he is deeply passionate
In his soul, he is grounded

He pulls me close to him, often
He runs his fingers over my cheeks, softly
He holds my hand as we walk, regularly
He fills my heart to the brim, effortlessly
He makes me want to open to him, easily
He places his hand on the small of my back in ways that ensure I feel completely protected and secure, even though I don't need it

He drives, carefully
He speaks, mindfully,
He creates, expansively

He loves, fully
He enjoys life, immensely

THIS MAN
Is respected, in his community
Is adored by his family
Is admired, by his peers
Is sought after, by celebrities, corporations and world leaders, yet accepts, understands and values all people no matter what title they may have been given by society

THIS MAN
Has talents, that have still to be tapped
Has qualities, that are increasingly being acknowledged
Has charisma, that is electric, magnetic and uplifting
Has charm, that is soothing
Has warmth, that is enriching
Has beliefs, that are enlivening

This man could be any man on the planet … and maybe he's mine … but one thing I know for sure, is that when a woman holds a vision so strongly, loves with her heart so fully, opens her mind so freely, prepares her body so completely, she can create him out of thin air.

CONFESSION #598 ...

I HAVE A LIST OF VALUES I LIVE UP TO MYSELF

Everyone else is off the hook ... ☺

CONFESSION #599 ...

I DON'T NEED MUCH

I don't need a man who is outrageously wealthy ... yet I do like to be with a man who believes that ANYTHING IS POSSIBLE.

I don't need a man who is incredibly handsome ... yet I do like to be with a man who has a SENSE OF STYLE AND CHARISMATIC CONFIDENCE.

I don't need a man who works hard for a living ... yet I do like to be with a man who knows how to ENJOY THE GOOD LIFE.

I don't need a man who lives in a fabulous house ... yet I do like to be with a man who will LET ME CREATE A HOME no matter where in the world we are.

I don't need a man who has an adventurous life ... yet I do like to be with a man who is eager to find someone to SHARE THE NICE STUFF WITH.

I don't need a man who's into fitness in a big way ... yet I do like to be with a man who knows that a happy heart, wholesome habits and positive attitude is the best foundation for a HEALTHY MIND, BODY AND SOUL.

I don't need a man with a perfect past ... yet I do like to be with a man who can REMEMBER THE BEST AND LET GO THE REST.

I don't need a man who has a lot of knowledge ... yet I do like to be with a man who ENJOYS THE PERSONAL GROWTH THAT ALL RELATIONSHIPS OFFER.

I don't need a man who's hoping to find the "right one" ... yet I do like to be with a man who will MAKE THE MOST WITH THE ONE HE CHOOSES.

CONFESSION #600 …

I HAVE NO REGRETS

And if YOU also knew what was on its way to you right now, you would not use one moment shedding a tear of regret, one instant thinking about what you would have done different, one minute worrying about what you've lost. You would only think about what there was to gain, only remember how much you have grown and only look with excited anticipation towards what is about to be the next great adventure of your entire life.

The next great adventure is NOT something we even need to think about. The next great adventure is always inspired from the heart, it is born from the contrast we have lived, it is molded out of all our secret desires, our wishes and passions and it flows to us swiftly, sweeps us away gently and holds us in its loving embrace from now unto eternity. As soon as we relax, in the very moment we allow it and in the instant we decide to say, "YES", I knew you were here waiting for me all along.

CONFESSION #601 …

I DON'T NEED TO BE ASSURED THAT THINGS WILL GO WELL IN THE FUTURE

I take one step at a time and turn in the direction that feels the best in this moment. This is where ALL my power is.

CONFESSION #602 …

I DON'T NEED A COMMITMENT TO MAKE A RELATIONSHIP WORK

I already made a commitment to myself to notice the most enjoyable aspects of everything, and then the most enjoyable aspects of my mate tend to rendezvous with me too.

CONFESSION #603 …

I DON'T NEED MY FRIENDS TO POSSESS CERTAIN QUALITIES

When it becomes a dominant quality in me, I notice it so much more in them too.

CONFESSION #604 …

I BLESS EVERYTHING, EVEN THE CONTRAST

I love to look back and wholly bless everything, that's brought us all to this moment.

CONFESSION #605 …

I REMEMBER MY MOST INTIMATE MOMENT

When I felt so incredibly loved and so wonderfully relaxed. I remember how delicious it was to taste my favorite food, to smell the sweetest scent, to touch the skin of a new born baby, to hear the laughter of children and the sweetness as I held the hand of my loved one during a tender moment. That's what THE PAST is really for; fond memories that propel us with love into tomorrow.

CONFESSION #606 …

I USE A SYSTEM

1. If it feels "off" I let it go.

2. If it feels good I give it my heart and soul.

CONFESSION #607 …

I'VE COME WITH GREAT PURPOSE

It isn't to save the planet (the planet doesn't need saving), it isn't to lead others to the light (everyone's been born with their Own Innate Guidance), it isn't to make a difference in the world (the world is intentionally designed to evolve through contrast), and it isn't to make myself a better person (each one of us is perfect, just as we are).

I've come for something far more profound that that!

I've come with great purpose, for joy, thrill and fun, with a mind, body and soul, to live, love and laugh, feeling all my emotions, and to expand the reality, that I want to see! With this purpose I know, I'm the creator of a life, that's just right for me.

CONFESSION #608 …

I LIVE A QUALITY LIFE

The quality of my life isn't defined by where I live, who I'm married to, how many assets I have or how successful my work is. The quality of my life is determined solely, by how intently I've chosen to focus my way towards feeling good, no matter what's going on right now.

CONFESSION #609 …

I'VE NEVER MADE A MISTAKE

I know that each experience has phenomenal value when I take the time to look for the advantages, to find something to laugh about, to talk about the upsides and decide what I'd prefer to be, do, feel, have and create, from now on.

*"There are no mistakes,
just different ways of looking at things."*

CONFESSION #610 …

I'VE GOT AN IMAGINARY BOYFRIEND

This is Elizabeth.
Elizabeth has a vivid imagination.
Be like Elizabeth
Use the most powerful tool to become a wife,
and imagine your dreams, into life … ♡

CONFESSION #611 …

I THINK THE CREATOR DESIGNED US PERFECTLY

I appreciate my clitoris most of all ... ☺

CONFESSION #612 …

IT'S IMPOSSIBLE TO OFFEND ME

I take EVERYTHING as a compliment!

Your attention to my perceived defects, faults, dysfunctions, failings and flaws says more about you than it does about me. Your attention to my magnificence says that you see clearly your own reflection shining brightly back at you.

CONFESSION #613 …

I HAPPILY THREW MY MORALS OUT THE WINDOW

And now use my gut instincts in each moment to determine if something feels right to me or not. I don't inflict my awareness on others or decide others are wrong for the choices they make, for in the very next moment, we have the chance to choose again the way of being that works best for each one of us.

Morals are created by "THINKING about the pain of the past" and take time to assess, analyze and rationalize. Gut instincts come from "FEELING the fullness of the present moment" and to know instinctually what to be, do, have, feel, create or choose next.

CONFESSION #614 …

I DON'T NEED OTHER PEOPLE TO GIVE ME WHAT I WANT

I trained my vibration instead, to me a match to what I love to receive.

CONFESSION #615 …

I AM SECURE WITH WHO I AM

I am so secure with who I am, that I allow my mate the freedom to be who he wants to be, see who he wants to see, do whatever feels right for him, and love and accept him anyway.

I love myself so much that I don't need it from others, yet I'm open to receiving whatever they feel inspired to give.

I feel so secure with who I am that I don't need someone to provide it in any particular way, yet I openly acknowledge and appreciate how secure they often make me feel anyway.

But most importantly, I AM TRUE TO MYSELF and know, if something feels good, it's right for me and how anyone else might feel about what I'm doing is their choice, not my responsibility.

CONFESSION #616 ...

I WOULD RATHER MY MATE FEEL FREE

To love in whatever way he chooses, than to feel obliged to love only me. I would rather my mate be true to himself in each moment, than to feel confined to a commitment he made in the past. I would rather remember that I'M SO AMAZING, that I'll cause him to remember, we can both be amazing together!

CONFESSION #617 …

I DIDN'T NEED SOMEONE ELSE TO "COMPLETE ME"

Instead, I like the idea of two people who already feel whole, content, happy and complete, coming together to expand the amazing lives they are already living.

CONFESSION #618 …

FREEDOM IS THE FOUNDATION OF REAL LOVE

If there are rules or restrictions of any kind, there is no real love, only expectation, insecurity and an attempt to control.

CONFESSION #619 …

THE BEST RELATIONSHIPS JUST EVOLVE

They aren't over-thought, planned, discussed, evaluated or based on compromise. They just happen naturally, when two people who already feel whole, happy and complete with the lives they're living, drift into each other's experience, often seemingly by accident.

But there are no accidents, just the powerful Law of Attraction that plays out perfectly when one or both become aware of a feeling of familiarity, knowing or deep comfort, like something they'd already lived in a distant imagining.

CONFESSION #620 …

MY IMAGINARY BOYFRIEND TAKES ME EVERYWHERE

CONFESSION #621 ...

I NEVER ASK FOR TESTIMONIALS

That's solicitation (trying to achieve a result), which pushes energy out.

I'M ABSOLUTELY CERTAIN OF MY VALUE

That's confidence (allowing the result), which attracts an abundance of similar energy to itself. So the testimonials, the comments and the compliments I receive are always real and raw and genuine and true. Thank YOU xox

CONFESSION #622 …

I'M A MAGNET

I attract all sorts of people. I'm a soother of many a soul, a beacon of light for some, a slice of entertainment for most. But I get to choose the ones that come close, the ones that come often, the ones who will play and the ones who will gently melt into my heart and stay.

CONFESSION #623 …

I LET LIFE UNFOLD

I've learned not to rush things, to force or even take score. I've learned not to "try" to make something happen or to push for even more. Now I simply ALLOW for things to unfold just as they will and trust the Universe knows what I really want and brings me something even better still. I always get the best results, when I relax and know my worth, and remember that I was an extension of God, from the moment of my birth.

CONFESSION #624 …

I CAN HANDLE PRESSURE

When I'm feeling stress, whether it is mental, emotional, situational or hormonal, THAT is the indication for me to take time out and nurture my own needs. How other people handle where I'm at and what I'm doing, is their own choice.

CONFESSION #625 ...

I LOVE LOUDLY

LOVING YOU ... is when I keep on knowing the goodness inside you, even when you can't see it, aren't feeling it, fail to show it or don't remember it yourself.

LOVING ME ... is when I remember, who we both really are no matter what's happening in our lives.

CONFESSION #626 …

I DON'T GET INVOLVED

I don't get involved in conversations that mute my joy.

I deliberately start conversations that spread good vibes.

CONFESSION #627 …

TIMING IS EVERYTHING

When I'm not feeling great, I know it's not the best time to try and sort things out, to engage in conversation, to complain or to share my troubles. Instead it's best to be quiet, to take time out, to let it all go and remind myself, I'll feel so much better, really soon.

"This too shall pass!"

CONFESSION #628 …

I'M DOING SOMETHING I'VE NEVER DONE BEFORE

I'm giving myself permission to stay angry as long as I bloody well feel like it … rarrrrrr… lol … Well that didn't last long did it … ☺

"There's nothing that shifts energy quicker, than accepting myself just as I am."

CONFESSION #629 ...

MY PRAYER FOR ALIGNMENT

When I have felt hurt, let me experience the stillness of peace. When I have felt hate, let the unkind thoughts slow down and cease.

When I have felt criticized, let me see that it was not about me. When I have felt confused, let me ask for greater clarity.

When I have felt powerless, let me remember God's on my side. When I have felt diminished, let love be my guide.

When I have felt disheartened, let memories of better times give me a lift. When I have felt sad, let tears of relief be my gift.

When I have felt troubled, let me sense the deepest calm. When I have felt angered, let me express it clearly, doing no further harm.

When I have felt resentment, let me seek forgiveness of self. When I have felt sick, let me be restored to wholeness and health.

When I have been doubtful, remember that "faith" helps me cope. When I have been depressed, let me be encouraged closer towards hope.

When I have been disrespected, may I find better ways to let it all go. When I have been judged; accept that is their prerogative and decide to not deal another blow.

When I have felt stressed; take a long deep breath of relief. When I have felt like a failure; affirm "inevitable success" as my belief.

When I have felt rejected, let a stronger connection to Source be my goal. When I have felt in bondage, let me give myself freedom to feel the fullness, of my own blessed soul.

CONFESSION #630 …

MY IMAGINARY BOYFRIEND IS SO REAL

He video calls several times a day. I am in heaven … ☺ … You're real. You're alive. You actually exist. Not only that … you're magnificent!

CONFESSION #631 ...

IT'S ALL GETTING CLOSER

- A BETTER IDEA is only a new thought away.
- IMPROVED HEALTH is only a relaxed moment away.
- INCREASED SUCCESS is only one more step away.
- BEING HAPPY is only a choice away.
- A NEW FRIEND is only a smile away.
- HELP is only a question away.
- RELIEF FROM STRESS is only a deep breath away.
- GETTING BACK ON TRACK is only a "change of focus" away.
- A MORE PROSPEROUS BANK BALANCE is only a belief away.
- RESOLVING A CONFLICT is only a "changed attitude" away.
- MOVING CLOSER TO OTHERS is only an outstretched hand away.
- FEELING MORE LOVE is only a heartbeat away.

CONFESSION #632 …

I SPEAK WELL OF OTHERS

COMPLAINING ABOUT SOMEONE doesn't change the other person, it just makes everyone who listens, feel worse.

PRAISING THEM for what they do well doesn't always change them either, but it has every chance to move all of us to feel so much better in the end, and feeling better is what I was wanting right from the start.

CONFESSION #633 …

I HELP MYSELF

The only thing that ever stopped me from loving myself was when I started compared myself to others.

The best attitude that led me towards self love was to give up worrying what others might think, to let go caring about how other people were feeling and to stop changing myself in response to where they are at.

The only thing that's ever stopped me from healing my body was when I was withholding something that someone else was wanting.

The best thing I did to help myself to feel whole and healthy again was to give it unconditionally.

CONFESSION #634 …

I MAKE PEACE WITH WHERE I AM

In the midst of turmoil I asked for help, with no clever words, no pledge to be better, no need to be perfect, just a simple request for assistance, with faith that it would be answered in the best way I'd allow it to come - and it was given almost immediately. But I was only able to hear it once I'd relaxed, made peace with what was happening, had a laugh or two, gave up the stress, stopped trying to control the outcome and opened up just a little to receiving Divine Guidance.

I didn't need to achieve a heightened state, I wasn't required to be filled with Love, I wasn't even close to genuine appreciation, but it taught me something very valuable - When I Ask, I Am Always Answered, and the answer came in a way that I was able to actually receive and one I could never possibly have orchestrated on my own.

CONFESSION #635 …

I HAVE THE POWER

- The power to choose where I place my attention.

- The power to decide which conversations I'll engage in.

- The power to take time out when I need it.

- The power to stop expecting myself and others to behave so perfectly.

- The power to think more positive thoughts, speak more supportive words and to give unconditionally from my heart, because it is who I intend to be.

CONFESSION #636 …

I LIKE INTIMACY ON ALL LEVELS

- Physical Intimacy is the closeness of bodies touching.

- Mental Intimacy is achieved through the sharing of personal details or experiences or beliefs about the self or another, with another.

- Emotional Intimacy is an understanding, a unity or a bond that's developed by getting through conflict together.

- Spiritual Intimacy is a natural connection that's formed with our own Source first and then transferred to another either prior to meeting or after intimacy has been experienced on any of the other levels. It can never be broken, just allowed or resisted.

CONFESSION #637 …

I ADORE OUR DIFFERENCES

FOR ME, A FEMININE WOMAN IS … someone who takes responsibility for her own happiness/radiance and never blames her man for how she is feeling. She takes time out to treat her feminine nature (with dance, shopping, lingerie, massage, beauty treats etc.) whenever she starts to feel a little resentful for all she has done, no matter what others might think. Because she is true to her own needs, she becomes someone who naturally acknowledges and appreciates the efforts he makes to plan, provide, produce or please her. She knows her own power is to playfully tease and seduce her man to get his attention and shows him OFTEN how important he is in her life.

FOR ME, A MASCULINE MAN IS … someone who knows what he wants and goes out and gets it (charismatic). He tends to his needs, passions, desires no matter what they might be (looking at porn, sports, spending time with his mates or in his cave re-charging etc.). He doesn't care what other people think (even his woman) BUT because he is always true to himself, he longs to give his life more purpose by choosing a suitable mate and expanding their existence together. He intrinsically knows his value and is proud of who he helps her become. He knows he has the power to get her attention by using romance and by reminding her often of the beauty, grace and purpose she adds to his life.

CONFESSION #638 ...

I USE MY FEMININE CHARM

Re-creating intimacy in a relationship has less to do with my mate and EVERYTHING to do with my attitude about him.

If I want to feel my feminine sensuality, I treat myself well FIRST, by doing whatever it is that makes me feel really good: taking time out, beauty treats, shopping, dancing, massage, walks in nature, letting myself fantasize, watch romantic movies, read erotica, buying myself flowers, lingerie or jewellery and pretending it's from my secret lover: whatever makes ME feel special.

I USE MY INSTINCTS TO BRING MY MAN CLOSER

1. Appreciate him.
2. Playfully tease him.
3. Let him be my hero.
4. Make him a significant part of my life.
5. Trust him.
6. Open to him.

CONFESSION #639 …

UNCONDITIONAL LOVE STARTS WITH ME

When I take as much time as I need to care for myself first, I have so much more of ME to share with others, and then when I'm ready; it is given with total joy, with gay abandon and without any need to receive something in return. That wonderful feeling of outpouring my own love is the best reward of all.

CONFESSION #640 …

I DECIDED TO LIGHTEN UP ON MYSELF

I don't have to always be the BEST me, the perfect mate, the guidance for others. I can just appreciate where I've come from, love who I am inside, acknowledge my own inner beauty and remember how magnificent I am most of the time, then my light will naturally start shining again and others may even find their way more clearly, because of where I've been.

CONFESSION #641 …

I'M IN SHOCK

I've just watched someone dress up as superman. Didn't see that coming! Is it a Bird? Is it a Plane? …. Nooooooo, it's my imaginary boyfriend again … ☺

CONFESSION #642 ...

I DECIDE WHAT I WANT TO BELIEVE

And then find all the evidence in the world to support it.

CONFESSION #643 …

MY DAYS ARE PERFECT

The perfect day isn't when everything goes to plan. The perfect day is when I follow my guidance, when I stay true to me and when I fulfill my intention to find humor, appreciation, happiness and love no matter what the heck happens.

CONFESSION #644 …

I'M ATTRACTIVE

MEETING THE RIGHT PERSON … is nice.

BEING THE RIGHT PERSON … is essential.

CONFESSION #645 …

I HAVE IT ALL

- RICH … is measured by the money that's available to me.

- WEALTH … is measured by how many assets I've accumulated.

- ABUNDANCE … is measured by how much freedom I claim.

- PROSPERITY … is measured by how incredibly, wonderfully, amazingly, awesomely good I feel right now whether I think I have enough money, freedom, assets or not.

CONFESSION #646 ...

MY FORMULA FOR A DEEPER UNDERSTANDING

1. ACCEPT that there are things I might not be aware of just yet.

2. TRUST that there's a good reason why each person is behaving the way they are.

3. BELIEVE that their actions are in some way benefiting me.

4. KNOW that God doesn't make mistakes.

CONFESSION #647 …

MY STRENGTH BENEFITS YOU

I'm not here to lower my standards so that you can feel adequate. I'm here to encourage you to reach for something that you've secretly wanted and never felt worthy to achieve, not just in material treasures but in emotional satisfaction and spiritual richness beyond your wildest dreams.

"I stay aligned with your dreams, not with your story!"

CONFESSION #648 …

MY WHOLE LIFE IS LIKE A HOLIDAY

This is Elizabeth.
Elizabeth is an innovator.
She doesn't just celebrate Australia Day, Birthdays, New Years, Long Weekends, Bar Mitzvahs, Labor Days and Christmas.
Be an innovator like Elizabeth
Take some time out,
treat yourself really well,
and pretend EVERY DAY is a holiday .. YES!

CONFESSION #649 ...

I'M LINING UP WITH WHAT I WANT

- I WANT IT!

- I'm enjoying the idea of it.

- I'm excited about it.

- I'm feeling it.

- I'm expanding the possibilities of it.

- I'm anticipating it.

- I'm beginning to realize it.

- I'm loving it.

- I'm appreciating everything that made me ask for it.

- I'm living it ... ☺

CONFESSION #650 ...

THESE THINGS I KNOW

- Life is meant to be fun.

- I profoundly influence my reality.

- The Universe responds to how I'm feeling.

- I attract or repel the very things I'm wanting with my thoughts, words and attitudes about them.

- If I didn't experience "what I don't want", I wouldn't have the thrill of heading towards "what I do want".

- I choose the mood of each day whether I'm aware of it or not.

- I decide if an event, circumstance or person will affect me in a negative way or if it will benefit me immensely.

- Where focus goes, energy flows.

- I can change a belief or habit that no longer serves me by changing my thoughts, words or actions.

- I empower myself when I stop worrying about what other people might think or say about me.

- No one can force their way into my experience unless I give them or their actions strong attention.

- When I do what's right for me, I have more to contribute to others.

- No event, circumstance or person is intrinsically good or bad! It's either accepted for what it is, or misunderstood completely.

- At the core of our being, we are *Love*.

CONFESSION #651 …

I FOUND THE SECRET TO AN ENCHANTED LIFE

Get happy *before* something good happens, and then it turns out even better.

CONFESSION #652 ...

I SAY "I LOVE YOU" ALL THE TIME

I say "I LOVE YOU" when I feel it! Not because I think I should, not because I believe I'm obligated and not because I want something in return. I say "I Love You" when I feel the warmth in my heart, when it's oozing from my soul and when it's almost impossible to contain.

CONFESSION #653 ...

I'M THOUGHTFUL

This is Elizabeth
Elizabeth is thoughtful
She wants to take this important moment to say ... I LOVE YOU!

Because Yesterday is gone,
Today is almost over ... and TOMORROW

... she's running off with her imaginary boyfriend ... ☺

CONFESSION #654 ...

I KNOW NO LIMITS

DON'T LIMIT YOURSELF ... by hoping to win the lottery, by wishing a particular job will be offered to you, by thinking a certain person is a perfect match ... there are SO many more ways for things to come.

I'VE MADE MORE MONEY ... from having faith and having fun, than from any "work" I've ever done.

CONFESSION #655 …

YOU DON'T NEED ME

Being a good mate or mentor or friend or parent or coach doesn't mean you need to continually boost the other person's confidence in themselves. It means you *have faith* they'll come into their own power with or without your support. Giving them space to discover what they're really capable of is often the quickest way to full self-empowerment.

> "I believe in you. I know you can do this. I trust you're finding the way that's right for you. I know Who You Really Are."

CONFESSION #656 ...

I LET MY HEART LEAD THE WAY

I never underestimate the calling of my heart. When I'm happy, when I'm flowing with love, when I'm feeling fully plugged in to life itself, my purest desires are heard around the planet ... and it comes, with unstoppable momentum as if it was meant to be here all along.

Sometimes I LAUGH so much I have to take time out to recover.

Sometimes the MONEY flows in so quickly that there's more than I have any sensible use for.

Sometimes I feel so LOVING for such a long stretch of time that it gets boring, and I deliberately create drama to shake things up a bit.

Sometimes I forget how much FUN it is to direct the course of my life and pretend there's something really serious going on here.

CONFESSION #657 ...

I'M FOCUSED

Whatever I'm giving my attention to now, has the power to influence the tone of my entire day.

CONFESSION #658 ...

I TELL STORIES

YOU "CAN" CHANGE THE PAST ... by giving the old story you've been telling a beginning, middle and ending that really lights your fire.

YOU "CAN" PROFOUNDLY INFLUENCE THE FUTURE ... by not telling the old story ever, ever, ever again.

YOU "CAN" CREATE THE FUTURE ... by telling a new story as if you're already living it, happily ever after.

CONFESSION #659 …

I LIKE TO TAKE ONE STEP AT A TIME

Slowing down, breathing deeper, getting some relief, finding peace with my thoughts, seeking the stillness inside, not aiming for any particular outcome, accepting that I am where I am, giving up trying to control circumstances and allowing the natural goodness of life to just flow

Solitude. In stillness, silence, calmness, peace and quiet. With softness, simplicity, dim lighting, open air and a gentle breeze. Finding balance, unity, alignment, Divine Assistance. Vibrating, meditating, revitalizing, nurturing, breathing, forgiving, accepting, opening, releasing, surrendering … being.

CONFESSION #660 …

HANDLING NEGATIVE MOMENTUM

- I BLESS the conflict even if I don't understand how I attracted it just yet.
- I CONTEMPLATE the potential benefits.
- I TELL MYSELF it's only temporary and will pass soon.
- I REMEMBER how things have worked out so well before.
- I'M TRUTHFUL about how I'm feeling in the moment.
- I ASK for what I "really" want and trust that it'll be done, one way or another.
- I AFFIRM "My life is expanding, and I'm going with it!"
- I STAY FAITHFUL to what feels "right" for me.
- I ALLOW OTHERS THE SPACE to discover their own truth.
- I STAND FIRM IN THE KNOWING of who they really are at their core.
- I STAND PROUD & STRONG IN THE KNOWING of Who "I" Am In My Heart.
- THEN I GIVE IT ALL TO GOD and get on with living, loving and laughing as much as I possibly can. There's relief in doing that!

CONFESSION #661 …

I'M NOT ALONE

Each day I remember that God's walking with me is a day spent in bliss, without a care in the world, knowing the goodness of my being, feeling perfectly alright no matter what's going on and remembering, that the joy of the journey isn't determined by who's watching my progress, but by who's walking alongside me.

CONFESSION #662 …

I DON'T TOLERATE ANYTHING

BEING TOLERANT is something you do when you don't know what else to do. BEING LOVING is what you do when you know who you really are.

CONFESSION #663 …

MY LIFE IS LIKE A FAIRYTALE

A fairytale doesn't need to be something you wait for, just like heaven doesn't need to be something you die to enter. It's something that begins in your mind, is felt in your heart and continues as long as you keep telling the story as YOU intend it to be.

CONFESSION #664 …

I LOVE BEING HOME

A love-filled home feels like peace, it feels like harmonious acceptance, it feels like everything is easier, it feels like a celebration of all that we are, it feels like great fun, it feels like happiness remembering all the good times, it feels like the excitement of imagining incredible things for our future, it feels like laughter and music and singing and delicious home-cooked food and picking freshly grown herbs and growing luscious tomatoes and sitting in the sunshine and getting rugged up for the cold and dancing in the rain and the occasional breakfasts in bed and walks on the beach and watching the sunset and getting up really early to revel in whatever today has in store for us.

CONFESSION #665 ...

THERE IS ANOTHER WAY

We won't wish for other people to be different; we'll focus our attention on what we really like and stimulate their better side instead.

We won't waste energy by remembering past failures, we'll find greater success in dreaming of a brighter, happier, more spiritually attuned future.

We won't keep talking about problems; we'll relax more and allow the solutions to be shown to us.

We won't worry about things that we have absolutely no control over, we'll open our hearts and minds to our own inner guidance and receive the answers to anything we could possibly wish for, right here.

We won't stress so much about changing the world and lack that feeling of comfort in our hearts, we'll find an abundance of fulfilment, love and joy as we look for endless things to be thankful for, just the way it is.

We won't work so hard to reach some apparently ideal destination, we'll trust that what we've asked for is coming, consciously take time out to breathe deeply into THIS moment and enjoy the journey so much more along the way.

We won't keep thinking that accumulating money and material objects will make us feel rich; instead we'll realize that inner alignment with the Source of Life is the best way to know true prosperity and create it more sustainably, meaningfully, purposefully, powerfully and joyfully, from the inside out.

We won't wait for our health, our mate or our circumstances to improve before we can feel better, we'll know real power as we consistently choose to experience harmony, serenity and stillness inside, no matter what might be happening outside.

In doing this, we'll remember the magnificent creators we really are and set everyone else free to remember their magnificence too.

CONFESSION #666 …

I'M SO HAPPY WITH WHO I AM

There comes a time when you stop trying to tell people who you are and what you do - YOU JUST BE YOU - you express you, you live as you, in all your glory, with all your uniqueness, through all your strong emotions, despite all your perceived flaws.

You know, the stunning Cindy Crawford once felt very insecure about the distinguishing mole above her lip; then it became her greatest trademark.

"Let your flaws turn into assets too."

CONFESSION #667 ...

I MADE A QUICK CHANGE

When that little bit of disappointment just crept in, I caught the thought quickly and relaxed straight back into FAITH.

- Faith that I'm still going in the right direction.
- Faith that I'll feel the impulse to know "what's next".
- Faith that I'm always being so wonderfully, clearly, divinely guided.
- Faith that the excitement about what's possible brings it directly into being.
- Faith in Frivolity and Fun and Joy and Beauty and Quality and Passion and Focus and Love.

*"Yeh, that's what's important.
Feeling good about where I am right NOW."*

CONFESSION #668 …

THE ANSWER IS INSIDE YOU

But it isn't found in frustration. It's impossible to see when you're disappointed. It can't be felt when you're worried. You won't know it when you're doubtful. It's never received while you're still asking or praying or questioning or taking score or looking for proof.

Get into a calm state, make peace with where you are, and trust that what you want is coming. Do this the best way you know how and your ACTIONS will then be inspired, the next WORDS you speak will be those of hope and the NEW IDEAS that flow, will guide you closer, easier, faster, to where you really intend to go!

CONFESSION #669 ...

I'M ENLIGHTENED

This is Elizabeth.
Elizabeth is enlightened.
Recently she's been getting lots of proposals from handsome eligible men.

Elizabeth just met Bill.
Be enlightened like Elizabeth.

Let the words, "I see a little silhouetto of a man" ... finally make sense to you too ... ☺

CONFESSION #670 …

I'M RIGHT

- Whenever I decide to feel honored, appreciated and supported, the evidence that I am, shows itself to me.
- Whenever I decide to feel loved, cherished and adored, the evidence that I am, shows itself to me.
- Whenever I decide to feel successful, wealthy and free, the evidence that I am, shows itself to me.
- Whenever I decide to feel any way I want, life proves me to be right.

"We have all been given that power: The power to consciously choose how we want to feel and to deliberately focus our attention in that direction!"

CONFESSION #671 …

I LEARN FROM EXPERIENCE

I've used all sorts of ridiculous excuses to break up a relationship in the past, but now I look for reasons to keep it together.

CONFESSION #672 …

IT'S INEVITABLE

It doesn't matter what I do or if I do nothing at all, I just can't stop the flow of wonderful things coming to me.

CONFESSION #673 …

I PAY ATTENTION

When I see something I don't like, I give it no attention at all! Instead I find the aspects that please me and give them all the time in the world.

CONFESSION #674 ...

I KNOW THE SECRET

- THE SECRET TO A LOVE FILLED LIFE ... Give without expecting anything in return.

- THE SECRET TO A HAPPY LIFE ... Please yourself!

- THE SECRET TO AN EXCELLENT LIFE ... Focus!

- THE SECRET TO A PEACEFUL LIFE ... Care more about being happy than about being right!

- THE SECRET TO A FULFILLED LIFE ... Fill yourself up with whatever makes you feel good and let the excess naturally shower over others!

- THE SECRET TO AN EASY LIFE ... Stop trying so hard!

- THE SECRET TO MANIFESTING ... Believe that good things are always knocking at the door, and just let them in!

CONFESSION #675...

WE HAVE SO MUCH TO GIVE

- When you're feeling good – enjoy it.
- When you think of something uplifting – share it.
- When you notice an aspect to compliment – say it.
- When you remember a funny joke – tell it.
- When you hear nice news about someone – spread it.
- When you need some relief – breathe into it.
- When you're trying too hard – relax it.
- When you find a blessing – expand it.
- When you feel a smile coming on – give it.
- When you're happy for no reason – express it.
- When you are feeling totally inspired – just do it.

"We have more to give than we know!"

CONFESSION #676 …

I SET BOUNDARIES

But the boundaries I set are for my benefit, not to condemn someone else's behaviour.

If I'm temporarily unable to find a person's most positive aspects when I think about them, I withdraw my attention from them completely until I can.

You see I love to FEEL GOOD more than anything else. I love feeling free, I love finding the best in others, I love to give love, share love, create love and make love because it's the most enjoyable experience I've ever known.

CONFESSION #677 …

I'M A DREAMER

I CAN ATTRACT ROMANCE just like I attract wealth, clients, friends, wellness or opportunities, by living in eager expectation of their arrival in my life and drawing them to me (This could be also be called Feeling Positive).

I CAN ALSO REPEL THE VERY THINGS I'M WANTING by complaining that I don't already have them, by noticing their absence, by doubting that it's possible, by being afraid to do something different, by feeling powerless to change, by blaming someone else for the predicament I'm in. (This could also be called Expressing Negativity And Doubt).

Everything that exists was first conceived in the imagination. DREAM BIG! Together we can be, do, have and create even more, than we've ever dreamed before.

CONFESSION #678 …

THERE ARE TWO TYPES OF ACTION I CAN TAKE

1. Action that's inspired, that feels good, that makes perfect sense and that's aligned with my intentions for my life.

2. Action done out of obligation, out of feeling guilty, feeling lack, feeling unworthy, feeling impatient, feeling angry or feeling any negative emotion which points me AWAY from what I really want for my life.

If I'm INSPIRED to take action and it makes me feel really good, anyone else's opinion becomes totally irrelevant, and NOTHING could possibly stop me. That's when I know I'm aligned with the future of my dreams, and not over-compensating for what I think I'm missing.

CONFESSION #679 …

I OVERCAME FEAR AND SET MYSELF FREE

I started to live totally, joyfully, adventurously, eagerly and whole-heartedly, when I accepted that we're ALL going to die …

… and I stopped worrying about the way it might occur, I stopped trying to prevent it from happening, I stopped making it the enemy, I accepted it as just another aspect of life and started to treat every experience as my very best friend - Now that's REAL FREEDOM!

I LOOK FORWARD TO DYING

I decided that death is a blessing instead of a curse. I believe good things will happen instead of expecting the worst. I imagine the peace and let go of the strife, I focus on what's wonderful and have a great life.

CONFESSION #680 …

I GAVE UP BEING CAUTIOUS - AND SET MYSELF FREE

I remember when I really started to ENJOY DATING, when I stopped being afraid that my heart might break, when I stopped talking about how I'd been hurt before, when I stopped and realized that the real tragedy would be if I never opened my mind, my heart and my soul to someone in an intimate way again ... and then I allowed myself to feel the depth of the love that is forever inside me just waiting to be shared.

CONFESSION #681 …

YOU CAN'T HURT ME

Every time I thought that someone hurt me, I can recall twice as many times they also loved me.

"When I focus on the negative I build a pathway to pain, when I focus on the positive I have so much more awareness to gain."

CONFESSION #682 …

ALL RELATIONSHIPS ARE SATISFYING

I don't need my mate's participation or agreement to have a satisfying relationship. I can make us both feel lighter by talking about the fun times we've had. I can make us both feel better by acknowledging the things he does that work for me. I can strengthen our bond by telling the story of how we first met or I can remind him how amazing he really is and draw out the goodness in both of us.

There only needs to be one leader, and I'm happy to be it. Not just because it might bring us closer, but because it feels really good to express the deep feminine wisdom that flows from inside me!

CONFESSION #683 …

I HAD TO DO THINGS DIFFERENTLY

When I realized how much power I have to create the life I desire, I was never again able to blame my mate, some event from the past or even karma or destiny for where I was at.

I STOPPED telling the old stories,
I STOPPED comparing myself to others,
I STOPPED sharing what wasn't working and
I STARTED to weave the fabric of life in a more colorful fashion. I make it fun, I laugh at myself, I turn it into a game, but I don't do it so I can change what's happening around me. I do it because it makes me feel good right now, and that's what really matters!

CONFESSION #684 …

I CAN BE WHATEVER I WANT TO BE

The universe isn't trying to teach me anything at all! It's just responding to how I am feeling. There's nothing I need to learn, but there's something I'm welcome to BE, hopeful, positive, trusting and with a sense of complete and utter faith that what I want, is on its way to me now!

CONFESSION #685 …

IT'S EASY TO CHOOSE

Whenever I have a choice to make, I choose the one that makes me shine, that turns me on, that widens my smile, that lifts my spirits, that warms my heart, that fills me with passion and lights up my life. Then I know an enjoyable result is assured, before I've even begun.

"There are times when making a choice might limit me, so in those moments, I decide, I truly can have it all!"

CONFESSION #686 …

I MAKE EXCELLENT DECISIONS

I've never made a bad decision, but it can sure seem bad when I dilute my energy with worry, with doubt, with fear, by blaming someone else, by making it wrong to change my mind or by assuming the Universe is trying to teach me a lesson. There's nothing to learn, but there's Something to be aware of; that *Staying Aligned* with any choice I make, is the most powerful decision of all.

CONFESSION #687 …

I HAVE A RELATIONSHIP WITH GOD

If you really believed in God, you would never be concerned about death, you would just live your life!

You'd be at peace with the world, and the variety of choices it holds. You'd be like Jesus who took time out to focus on living in a way that was right for him.

You'd know there are no villains and no victims. You'd be like Jesus who accepted each and every one of us, just as we are.

You'd know there is no disease or disability or disaster that cannot be overcome. You'd be like Jesus and see beyond it until people believed so much in your vision, that they got up from their wheelchairs and walked.

CONFESSION #688 …

I'M A PLEASURE SEEKER

I get as much pleasure from tasting the contents of a jar of home-made apricot jam as I do from selling another book. From feeling the tingling through my body as I take another really deep breathe as I do from checking the increase of my bank balance. From smelling the sweet scent of a freshly opened rose as I do from noticing the financial success I've already achieved.

And in those moments I knew, real success is not only contained in the things I've achieved, it's found so much more profoundly in how good I'm feeling about myself, right now!

CONFESSION #689 …

I WORK WITH THE LAW OF ATTRACTION

This is Elizabeth.
Elizabeth is focused.
Sometimes she gets tempted to talk about her own problems or tell the world how sick she's been.
But Elizabeth is into the Law Of Attraction. She knows that everything she talks about, just GETS BIGGER!
Be focused like Elizabeth.
Talk about Bills' penis instead … ☺

CONFESSION #690 …

EVERYTHING YOU DO BENEFITS ME

I'm that powerful!

CONFESSION #691 …

I LISTEN TO MY OWN INNER TRUTH

I once believed what I read in the media, that the earth was in serious turmoil, that Monsanto was a company worth fighting against, that the "banksters" were trying to rule the world, that most musicians were drug addicts, that celebrities had lives worth gossiping about, that politicians were really idiots … ☺ … then I decided to get off the bandwagon and get a life of my own!

I once believed what I read in romantic fiction, that finding the right person to love me was the clear destination. But I wanted to choose different goals to the rest of the population, and stop anticipating loss, pain and hyperventilation. So I started to love ME and my own creation, and gravitated instead, towards things that felt like jubilation. I also remembered, drama is deliberately used to cause sensation, because, "If it hurts it isn't real love - it's expectation!"

CONFESSION #692 ...

I AM FULFILLED

EMOTIONALLY SECURE ... is feeling so sure of who you are and what you have to offer that you accept your perception of what's manifesting around you is a direct indication of how you're really feeling inside.

EMOTIONALLY DEPENDENT ... is needing other people to behave or communicate in a certain way so you can feel secure in a relationship, in a work environment, in a family unit or in general day to day life.

EMOTIONALLY FULFILLED ... is knowing that God as my Source is calling forward the best of everything, no matter how it might appear at the time. In this state, all emotions, all behaviors, all expressions are not only acceptable, but necessary, to experience the height, width, depth and breadth of what an exhilarating life is really mean to be like.

CONFESSION #693 ...

I USE MY INTUITION

IF IT FEELS GOOD ... It's guidance! What I'm thinking, saying and doing is perfectly aligned with how I've imagined my life to be.

IF IT FEELS BAD ... It's also guidance! Something I'm thinking, saying or doing is not aligned with what I really want for my life.

CONFESSION #694 ...

I KNOW THE BENEFIT OF CONTRAST

- Out of discomfort, a way to be more comfortable is conceived.

- Out of rejection, a way to accept our own uniqueness is attained.

- Out of hurt, a way to feel soothed is found.

- Out of want, a way to achieve our hearts desire is defined.

- Out of pain, a way to get relief is sought.

- Out of death, a way to prolong quality of life is produced.

- Out of disaster, a way to provide safer conditions is discovered.

- Out of all contrast comes the ability to expand, to grow, to evolve and to give life its ultimate purpose, to continue to infinity and beyond.

CONFESSION #695 …

I USE MY TIME WISELY

I don't want to waste a minute thinking about the worst that can happen. I take all the time in the world, to imagine the best …☺

CONFESSION #696 …

NOTHING NEEDS TO CHANGE

One of my greatest joys is when I find my own alignment again, without anything or anyone else needing to change.

CONFESSION #697 …

I GET IN THE ZONE

I once thought that it was the action I took that got the biggest results. But now I know nothing beats "Being In The Zone" before I make a decision, before I take a phone call, before I get involved in a deep conversation, before I jump in the car to drive, before I write the next post, before I reach for comfort food, before I have sex, before I do anything important at all.

"Feeling that oneness with the Source inside me first, gives the best results of all."

CONFESSION #698 …

I RELAX AND TRUST

The more important something is to me, the harder it is to achieve. The more relaxed and trusting I am about it, the easier it comes to me.

CONFESSION #699 …

THINGS KEEP GETTING BETTER

Things get better whenever I stay silent instead of complain, as I release the bad but let the good memories remain. Every time I overlook an issue to see the deeper intent, when I take a moment to understand what the other person really meant.

Things get even better as I learn to trust, that there's nothing I need do, even when I assume that I must. It happens with each thought I improve, with each wrong that I right, when I look towards peace instead of turning to fight, and as I step through the darkness and shine my light bright.

CONFESSION #700 …

I LIVE LIFE ON MY TERMS

- I feel completely FREE, not allowing the constraints, judgments, opinions or expectations of others, limit who I know myself to be.
- I never aim for less than what I truly DESIRE.
- I GIVE what I want, when I want, to whoever I want, as often as I want and I'm open to RECEIVE as well.
- I tell the TRUTH to myself no matter how much I think it might hurt.
- I search for the POSITIVE ASPECTS in everything.
- I ACCEPT we are all doing the very best we can, no matter what crazy behaviour we sometimes demonstrate.
- I live with INTEGRITY and won't ever pretend to be less than the incredible person I know I am just so someone else can feel better.
- I ADORE myself, but if others don't, that's OK too.
- I'm OPEN to find happiness, ecstasy and bliss in as many places as I can.

- I APPRECIATE everything I've already been given … even if I might not understand its benefits at the time.
- I'm THANKFUL for the surprises and delights I'm about to receive.
- I choose to find something to LAUGH about every day.
- I do whatever it takes to BE TRUE to me.
- I IMAGINE myself living the most enchanting life and allow the Universe to orchestrate the finer details.
- I can EXPERIENCE the darkest despair and then rise from the ashes, knowing my Higher Self is always shining a light for me.
- I LOVE unconditionally, without expecting anything in return.
- I find as many reasons as possible to PRAISE myself and others.
- I intend to be an UPLIFTING influence in the lives of those I touch.
- I look for the MAGNIFICENCE in nature and the BEAUTY in people all around me.
- I KNOW my birthright is to be Whole, Healthy and Wealthy.
- I feel my deepest PASSIONS and follow them with gentle persistence.
- I LISTEN to the calling of my soul and surrender to it completely.

CONFESSION #701 ...

IT'S ALL ABOUT ME

- When I assume someone else is the problem - it's really me!

- When I decide someone isn't giving me what I need - it's about me not meeting my own needs!

- When I think someone else should change - it's really me that needs to change my attitude!

- When I focus on what someone else has done wrong - it's really me who's focusing in the wrong direction!

- When I believe someone's stopping me from having what I want - it's really me preventing good things from coming!

- Everything starts, continues and ends with the attention I keep giving it - period!

CONFESSION #702 …

I HAVE GOOD REASONS

THERE'S ONLY ONE GOOD REASON TO STAY ... because it feels good.

THERE'S ONLY ONE GOOD REASON TO LEAVE ... because it feels better.

There's really only one good reason for me to do anything at all. When I do something in the hope I'll get something in return, I'm setting myself up for disappointment. When I do something just because it makes me feel good, I win every time.

CONFESSION #703 …

I NEVER FEEL BAD

I don't feel bad about anything that's happened in the past. The only thing that can make me feel bad afterwards, is when I keep making some aspect of it "wrong". I don't feel bad about anything that might happen in the future either. I make the best use of each creative moment by projecting my "desires" into the Universe, not my fears!

CONFESSION #704 …

I'M CREATING A FANTASTIC FUTURE

Instead of trying to fix something that's gone wrong today, I use my time wisely now, to imagine how it will be so much better next time around. Instead of reacting to the present, I pre-pave my way into the future.

CONFESSION #705 ...

I FOUND IT ALL INSIDE ME

I FOUND SATISFACTION INSIDE ME ... when I stopped comparing myself to others.

I FOUND FREEDOM INSIDE ME ... when I stopped worrying what someone else might think.

I FOUND EASE INSIDE ME... when I stopped trying so hard to be perfect, and right, and good.

I FOUND BETTER HEALTH INSIDE ME ... When I stopped looking outside to find a cure for illness and started remembering my natural inner wellness.

I FOUND MORE JOY INSIDE ME ... when I stopped doing things out of obligation and started doing them because it made ME feel good.

I FOUND SOLUTIONS INSIDE ME ... when I stopped reinforcing the problem and just "allowed" the solution.

I FOUND FULFILLMENT INSIDE ME ... When I started to fill myself up first and found out I had so much more to give to others.

I FOUND PEACE INSIDE ME ... when I stopped making other people's choices wrong, when I let them walk their own path and when I just concentrated on enjoying mine.

I FOUND BETTER RESULTS BEGAN INSIDE ME ... when I started to imagine everything going really, really well.

I FOUND THAT LOVE CAME SO EASILY TO ME ... when I stopped looking at what others were giving and OPENED MYSELF UP to truly receiving.

I FOUND THAT MONEY CAME SO EASILY TO ME ... when I stopped trying to find ways to "make it" and just looked for more ways to "have fun".

I FOUND THAT SUCCESS CAME SO EASILY TO ME ... when I stopped working for a living and started playing with my life.

What I wanted was here all the time.

CONFESSION #706 ...

I'M AN EXPERT

This is Elizabeth.
Elizabeth is smart.
When she hears about the latest new internet trend, she doesn't immediately run off and do a webinar about how to make money out of it, create a Facebook page and ask everyone to like it or try to get all her friends to attend a workshop about it.
Be smart like Elizabeth.
She just sticks with what she's an expert at,
A Study Course On Relationships ... because she's had so many! ... ha ha ha ha ha ha ... ☺

CONFESSION #707 …

I LOVE A SATISFYING RESULT

I get better results by deciding how I want to experience life, by choosing a more loving thought, a more empowering meaning, a more uplifting conversation, a more life enhancing belief, a more uplifting mood.

I choose the results I get each day, just like I choose what I will eat for breakfast. NOT choosing what I want is still choosing, to leave it in the lap of the gods. But I can lighten up on myself and everyone else, life still works out, whether I consciously choose, or not!

CONFESSION #708 ...

I CHOOSE FUN

Fun is something we can look for, something we want to have or something we can associate with an activity. But, fun is not something that just happens, it is not a characteristic of any particular event or action - it is a state of mind. One activity we enjoyed in the past may lose its appeal if we are "Having A Bad Day".

"Fun is something we create, stimulate or make a decision about, ALL in our minds."

CONFESSION #709 …

NO MATTER WHAT'S GONG ON, I CAN CHANGE HOW I FEEL

If I want to feel better:

I Change my diet
I Change my focus
I Change my breathing
I Change who I'm spending time with
I Change my environment
I Change the way I'm communicating
I Change my shoes … true … lol
I Change what I think it all means
I Change the direction I'm sleeping
I Change my proximity to the problem
I Change my clothes
I Change my body posture

But most importantly, I Change the story I'm telling about what's happened, and allow a brand new point of attraction to emerge.

CONFESSION #710 …

THE HARDEST THINGS CAN BE THE MOST REWARDING

TO ACCEPT, even when I felt like condemning.

TO LOVE, even when my heart was hurting.

TO BELIEVE IN MYSELF, even when others doubted my abilities.

TO FIND STRENGTH, even when all hope was lost.

TO EXPRESS MY TRUE FEELINGS, even when I was afraid of the outcome.

TO GO FOR WHAT I REALLY WANTED, even though it seemed unreasonable.

TO TRUST MY INNER GUIDANCE, even though I couldn't see the benefit.

TO ALLOW MYSELF TO BE VULNERABLE, even when I was crying out for certainty.

TO HAVE FAITH THAT EVERYTHING IS WORKING OUT PERFECTLY, even if it seemed far from the truth.

TO KNOW IT'S OK TO BE WHERE I'M AT, because this too will change;

- even if I don't know the answer,
- even if I haven't found clarity,
- even if I'm not yet aware of the solution,
- and, even if I do nothing at all.

CONFESSION #711 …

I'M HAPPY ANYWAY

The quickest way to be happy is to stop waiting for my mate, my health, my boss, my level of wealth or my government to change, before I can be happy, and just choose to find it inside myself anyway.

CONFESSION #712 …

I REACH MY GOALS IN AN INSTANT

The quickest way to reach my goals, is to imagine, to believe, to trust, to act as if, it's already here. Relax. It's coming. It's happening. It's certain. It's inevitable.
It's DONE!

CONFESSION #713 …

I WORK WITH MY FEELINGS

The quickest way to stop feeling stuck is to accept where I am, admit how I'm really feeling and then decide how I want to feel instead.

CONFESSION #714 …

I GIVE TO MYSELF FIRST

The quickest way to break up a relationship, is to expect my mate to give me something that I'm not even giving myself.

CONFESSION #715 …

PEOPLE FALL IN LOVE WITH ME

The quickest way to get someone else to fall in love with you, is to adore, love, nurture and appreciate yourself so much, that it doesn't matter if they do or not.

CONFESSION #716 ...

I ONLY MAKE AGREEMENTS I AM WILLING AND INTEND TO KEEP

The quickest way to lose trust in a relationship is to make an agreement and then break it.

CONFESSION #717 …

I AM TRUSTED

The only way to gain trust in a relationship is to make an agreement and then keep it. Make an agreement and then keep it. Make an agreement and then keep it. Make an agreement and then keep it. Make an agreement and then keep it. Make an agreement and then keep it. Make an agreement and then keep it. Make an agreement and then keep it. Make an agreement and then keep it. Make an agreement and then keep it.

Or decide, to not make any agreements at all and simply live true to how I feel in each moment.

"The most important relationship is the one between My Self and My Source."

CONFESSION #718 …

I CAN DO SO MUCH FOR MYSELF

THE "CERTAINTY" I thought I needed from others so I could feel secure, I found inside myself, by simply being more selective about what I give my attention to.

THE "VARIETY" AND DRAMA I created so I could feel more alive, has been replaced by allowing myself to feel and express ALL my emotions, for no reason at all.

THE "SIGNIFICANCE" I once craved so that I could feel important, has been replaced by a raw desire to just be myself, no matter what other people might think.

THE "LOVE & CONNECTION" I thought my mate should be giving me, I decided to start giving to myself.

CONFESSION #719 ...

I'M NOT QUALIFIED

I'm not qualified to do anything important, especially being a parent. I just started doing stuff and then the qualifications became irrelevant. Experience is the best teacher, and the right people, the best opportunities, the most appreciative clients, customers and co-creators, just show up.

CONFESSION #720 …

NOTHING STAYS THE SAME FOREVER

If I'm feeling bad, I don't need to worry, I know it'll all be over soon!

CONFESSION #721 …

WHEN A GUY REALLY LIKES A GIRL

He'll dig deeper, reach further, fly higher, just to have a chance to be with her. He's virtually unstoppable … ☺

WHEN A GIRL "REALLY" LIKES A GUY

It makes little difference to the dynamics of the relationship. But if she "Really Loves Herself", it makes all the difference in the world … ♡

CONFESSION #722 ...

I ONLY DO WHAT I WANT TO DO

Each day I make two lists.

1. What I intend to do today.

2. What I am giving to The Universe to manage for me.

Wisdom is, knowing what I can control, letting go what I don't want to do and being willing to admit the truth about it. The Universe has never failed to deliver whatever I have asked for in the moment I've released the resistance to receiving it!

CONFESSION #723 …

I'VE TRAINED MYSELF WELL

For every fault I think I have, I take the time to find at least three more positive aspects to compliment myself on.

1. What have I done well today?

2. What can I find to be pleased with today?

3. What do I appreciate about myself today?

When I don't like something about myself, I feel separate to the rest of the world and no one else can possibly live up to my expectations.

But when I really love and accept myself, I feel connected to the entire Universe and everyone else seems fabulous, just the way they are too.

CONFESSION #724 …

THE TIMING IS PERFECT … REALLY!

There's never any need to stress and worry, because that just slows the whole process down and gives me more things to stress and worry about.

I always know when to take action. When I'm feeling really good, when the action is inspired, when it seems like the next most sensible step, when it feels totally compelling and when a thousand raging bulls couldn't stop me from proceeding.

CONFESSION #725 …

I DON'T NEED TO CHANGE WHAT YOU THINK ABOUT ME

It's not my job to change what you think about me. It's my job to change HOW I FEEL about what you think about me!

CONFESSION #726 …

I'M HIGH ON LIFE

HIGH ACTION … when I work and work and work, intently focused on achieving a task and reveling in it.

HIGH INSPIRATION … when I write and write and write, gently allowing words to flow through me and thriving on it.

HIGH ON LOVE … when I live and love and laugh, passionately focused on my mate and adoring him.

Hi-BERNATION … when I take time out to bring myself back to center, so I can give as much as I possibly can, in any of the other areas I choose.

CONFESSION #727 ...

I CAN TOTALLY UNDERSTAND WHY PEOPLE DO WHAT THEY DO

Expressing anger, rage, revenge, blame, irritation, disappointment, annoyance or doubt isn't negative if it makes someone feel better in the moment ... quite the opposite ... anything that brings relief is always a step in the right direction. I've learned it's best to let go the judgment and just get out of the way. It'll all be over soon.

CONFESSION #728 …

I CAN GET HAPPY REAL QUICK

WANT TO KNOW HOW I GET HAPPY QUICKLY? … Mind my own business.

WHAT IS MY BUSINESS? … My thoughts. My focus. My words. My perceptions. My desires. My alignment. My willingness to be true to me.

CONFESSION #729 …

I KNOW THAT ANYTHING IS POSSIBLE

If I can conceive it - it's possible.
If I can imagine it - it's happening.
If I can believe it - it's on its way.
If I can just relax and let it come to me
- it's done!

CONFESSION #730 …

I'M NOT HERE TO MAKE A DIFFERENCE

I don't care if I make a difference in the world or not! All I care about is that I'm having as much fun, feeling as much joy and sharing as much love as I possibly can.

I never ask, "What will give me the best results?" I ONLY ask "What will bring me the greatest pleasure?" And when I'm sharing the fullness of Who I Am, we all thrive.

CONFESSION #731 ...

I SEE UNCONDITIONAL LOVE EVERYWHERE

Ready to be acknowledged in any moment.

- It's the part of me that gets totally energized when I've opened up to another solution.
- It's the part of me that overflows with an understanding of what someone else might be going through.
- It's the part of me that feels my heart flutter just thinking about my lover, just listening to the laughter of children or just witnessing the wide smile of a stranger.
- It's the part of me that accepts myself totally, even if I "think" I've done something wrong.
- It's the part of me that lightens up a seriously boring conversation.
- It's the part of me that knows I'm worthy and remembers that everyone else is too.
- It's the part of me that gets up in the middle of the night to comfort a crying baby, not because I feel obligated, but just because I can!

- It's the part of me that gives, just because it feels really, really good.
- It's the part of me that sees the best in whatever is happening.
- It's the part of me that loves, even when the other does not.
- It's the part of me that feels completely connected to the "oneness".
- It's the part of me that gets so much pleasure from smelling freshly baked bread, walking barefoot on the sand, patting the cat, waking up next to my mate each morning, and feeling such deep appreciation to be alive, that it spills out and showers over others.

CONFESSION #732 …

I LOVE BEING ME

I'm discovering the power of who I am. By staying true to myself, by asking for what I want, by caring about how I feel, by tending to my own needs first, by reaching for my dreams, by believing that anything is possible, by not letting things get me down, by allowing myself to admit it when they do, by accepting people no matter what side they show and by loving them for who I know they really are anyway.

"Being Loved Unconditionally is what makes people climb the walls the most."

CONFESSION #733 ...

I HAVE A BIG HEART

This is Elizabeth.
Elizabeth is wise.
She knows that it's popular to wear shorter skirts that show off her beautiful legs, and to smile a lot to let everyone know she's happy. But Elizabeth has discovered that "Being Real" is getting her lots of offers now too. Men are finding it easier to see right through to her heart.
Well, once they get past her glorious boobs that is ... ☺

CONFESSION #734 …

I LIVE WITH INTEGRITY

Integrity is, being true to your own beliefs, wishes, desires and dreams, without being influenced by what others might think, say or do. Integrity is a personal matter. Deciding that someone else is not in integrity is a judgment based on how WE believe they should behave. It couldn't be further from the truth.

CONFESSION #735 …

I ACCEPT EVERYTHING AS IT IS NOW

I don't wish for other people to be different, I focus my attention on the aspects I prefer and stimulate their better side instead.

I don't waste energy by remembering my past failures; I find more success in dreaming of a brighter future.

I don't keep talking about problems; I relax and allow the solutions to come through me.

I don't wait for situations to change before I can have a feeling of comfort in my heart. I find an abundance of peace as I look around for endless things to appreciate instead.

I don't expect other people to make me happy, I feel incredible as I consistently choose to experience happiness inside, no matter what is happening outside.

In doing this, I remember the magnificent creator I really am and set everyone else free to remember their magnificence too.

CONFESSION #736 …

I WANT YOU TO BE HAPPY

I WANT YOU TO BE HAPPY ... but if I sacrifice my happiness so you can have yours, I've not only encouraged you to give your power to me, I've given away my own - and we both lose.

I WANT YOU TO BE HAPPY ... and when I fill myself up first, when I honor my own feelings in each moment, when I'm nurturing my own needs at any time, I have so much more to shower over you - and we both win.

I WANT YOU TO BE HAPPY ... and when I'm being true to me, I'm showing you how to be true to YOU. When I'm trusting you'll find your own way too, I'm treating us as two whole individuals - who can do nothing else but thrive together.

CONFESSION #737 …

THERE ARE THINGS I JUST DON'T NEED

I don't bother with HEALING. Healing energy tends to move slowly because the focus is on what needs to be fixed.

I resonate more with WHOLENESS. Energy that vibrates at the frequency of God.

I don't bother with GRATITUDE. Gratitude tends to contain elements of whatever needed to be overcome.

I resonate more with APPRECIATION. Appreciation is energy that vibrates around the frequency of love. The difference in emotion when those words are even spoken is remarkable.

I don't bother with FORGIVENESS anymore either. When I don't pass judgment in the first place, forgiving someone is never necessary.

I never need COURAGE. When I wait until I reach the point that I THINK things will go well, I EXPECT positive results and I

BELIEVE everything will work out (even if I don't know how) no action ever needs courage, it's just purely inspired from the heart and makes perfect sense to my mind, both at the same time.

Courage is only needed by those who take action before they've prepared themselves vibrationally. It still works, but it's backwards, and nowhere near as easy to achieve. I don't need to push myself to be courageous to achieve a result - I stand easy in my faith and attract it.

I never need DETERMINATION. That's OK for those who like to work hard. Instead I use faith, and let things all happen easily.

CONFESSION #738 …

I'VE WRITTEN MY MARRIAGE VOWS

IN FAITHFULNESS AND BEFORE GOD, I PROMISE THESE THINGS:

I promise that I will do whatever it takes to maintain my alignment with Source so that I can give you the very best of me AND have as much fun as I possibly can … lol … what a price to pay.

I promise to be true to myself and that I'll encourage you to be true to what's right for you too, even if that means you need to break, rewrite or change a previous intention.

I want the best for you at all times and I won't allow anything less. No promise, no vow, no pledge you make to me should ever hold you in a place of discontent.

I grant you the right to follow your dreams, actually, not only do I grant you the right, I insist you claim that right, even if that means you need to do it without me.

I promise that I will help stir up enough trouble that we will both expand enormously. (Courtesy of Abe Hicks - and my playful side absolutely loves that concept).

I promise to never blame you for how I'm feeling.

I promise to move through my stuff as quickly, gracefully and elegantly as possible so I can show up in all my glory right next to you every day of our lives.

IF IT IS YOUR WISH TOO, I OFFER YOU THESE THINGS:

- I offer to contribute my finest skills to your life in the most meaningful ways.
- I offer to regularly wrap you in the warmth of my heart.
- I offer to stimulate you with the ever expanding wisdom from my mind.
- I offer to enliven you with the energized spirit expressed through my emotions.
- I offer to share with you the openness, willingness, pleasure and comfort of my body.
- I offer to connect with the pure desire burning passionately inside our souls.

NO MATTER WHAT HAPPENS NOW OR IN THE FUTURE:

I THANK YOU for being so intensely loving, charismatic, romantic, handsome beyond description, sexy, tasteful and energetically present, so that I could experience what it's like to be turned on emotionally, mentally, physically and spiritually all at once by another human being.

I THANK US for molding ourselves into two whole, heart strong, empowered, spiritually connected and independently happy individuals before we got together, which gives us the biggest opportunity to share more fun, more peace, more joy, more laughter, more life, more ecstasy and more love together, than we could ever dream of creating alone.

I THANK GOD that our two worlds collided at just the right time, with enormous momentum, in an incredibly magical way and with such impeccable precision that nothing short of Divine Alignment could have possibly made it happen.

CONFESSION #739 ...

I DON'T WANT YOU TO MAKE A COMMITMENT TO ME

I've already made a commitment to myself that I will do what feels right for me; without expecting anything in return. And you will know the same empowerment that I know when you choose to make your next commitments to yourself too.

"I'm confident with who I am and I give you the freedom to be more of who you are too!"

CONFESSION #740 …

YOU DON'T HAVE TO BE PERFECT

I can lighten up a little and give each of us the benefit of the doubt.

"I know that we're all doing the best we can in each moment!"

CONFESSION #741 …

I DON'T CARE IF YOU HAVE FAULTS

While I might notice some things about you that I don't wish to focus on, I don't need to point them out, ask you to change or suggest you improve anything at all. I'd rather spend my time wisely and expand on the uplifting aspects that make me feel good, and bring out the best in both of us.

"When I focus on the positive aspects of you, I feel better about me too!"

CONFESSION #742 …

I DON'T NEED YOU TO LOVE ME

I don't need you to care. In fact, I don't need anything from you at all. It only takes ONE of us to love unconditionally and lead us both out of the darkness and into the light.

"I'm a leader!"

CONFESSION #743 ...

IT DOESN'T MATTER IF YOU DISAGREE WITH ME

I can always look for our similarities, not our differences, and when I stop trying to prove a point and just let the issue go, it helps us both realize quicker that we are really wanting the same things underneath it all.

"At our core, we are pretty much the same!"

CONFESSION #744 …

IT'S IMPOSSIBLE TO DISAPPOINT ME

I don't need you to be different so I can feel loved, so I can be happy, so I can find peace. I give those things to myself as the greatest gift of all.

"I love me!"

CONFESSION #745 …

IT'S IMPOSSIBLE TO DESERT ME

I don't force anyone to make a promise and never set them free. Freedom is the foundation for openness, for truth, for integrity and the very soul of everlasting relationships.

I have no rules for me; I have no rules for you. I prefer to take each precious moment to decide what I will do, and feel the freedom that's known when, To Myself I Am True!

CONFESSION #746 ...

YOU'RE ALWAYS FORGIVEN, EVEN BEFORE YOU ASK

I've never judged your behaviour as wrong to start with. Each person is doing the best they know how with the life they're living and if I don't like something you've done, I can change my perception of it, change what I think it all means or change the position you hold in my life. It's my job to ensure my own needs are met; it's not your job to make me dependent on you.

CONFESSION #747 …

YOU CAN'T DO ANYTHING WRONG THAT WOULD TAKE MY LOVE AWAY

Closing my heart and mind to you hurts more than anything I've ever known, but keeping my heart and mind open to an expanded version of love (no matter how you're behaving, no matter where you're at, no matter who you're with), stimulates my soul more than anything else can ever do.

*"I don't love you because you deserve it;
I love, because it's who I am!"*

CONFESSION #748 …

I DON'T NEED YOU TO HAVE THE SAME BELIEFS AND VALUES

After a while "sameness" just gets boring. It's diversity that makes me grow, that calls me to be better, that opens my eyes to what's infinitely possible. Yet it's inevitable that as I live my life with this attitude, harmony will more naturally occur, whether we choose to move forward and create a future together or move onward to new beginnings.

"Accepting our differences helps me grow stronger and connects me more to Who I Really Am!"

CONFESSION #749 …

IT DOESN'T MATTER IF YOU HAVE AN ADDICTION

The only time it does affect me is when I give it more power by noticing it, resenting it, hating it, talking to others about it, fighting against it or having any strong emotion about it at all.

"The key to a happy life isn't to manipulate the conditions around me so I can feel better, the key is to change the meaning I give it and find happiness, no matter what's going on!"

CONFESSION #750 …

I DON'T CARE WHAT YOU DO OR SAY

When I keep anticipating the best responses from you, pretty soon, without any effort at all, you show me how amazing you really are, you show me how adaptable you can be, you show me how wide you can open your mind and you show me how enormously you can grow your heart, because that's who you really want to be too.

"I imagine the best in you, not because you deserve it, but because I'm worth it!"

CONFESSION #751 ...

YOU DON'T NEED ME TO LOVE YOU

Did you know that you are already loved for who you are, without needing to change, without needing to prove you're worthy, without needing to get fit, give up addictions, find the best job, choose the right religion, worship the one true God, subscribe to meditation, confess your sins, right your wrongs, forgive your ex's, please your parents, follow the rules ... without expressing gratitude, without feeling loving, without any requirements at all?

Inside your own heart is a place where total and utter unconditional love resides. You can touch it with your hand, feel it through a deeper breath, sense it in the stillness, see it as the light, taste it through a smile, call it in your darkest hour and know it as the essence of life itself.

"You're never alone. Your own inner-YOU is always here to remind you, how precious you really are."

CONFESSION #752 …

I FOCUS ON WHAT I PREFER TO EXPERIENCE

- I love having fun. Let's do more of that.

- I thrive on uplifting conversations. Let's have more of those.

- I get a buzz when I find solutions for my challenges. Let's relax and allow more of them.

- I have a passion for business. Let's expand into new, progressive and stimulating horizons there.

- I am excited about living fully. Let's accept the past, take time out to appreciate what we've already been given and boldly move towards the most insanely intoxicating future we can imagine.

- I adore feeling good. Let's choose to be light-hearted, find our alignment at least once every day, value the people around us fully, enjoy the simple things in life more often and raise the vibrations of the entire Universe along the way.

- I cherish the deepest intimacy, closest connection and warmest love in our relationship. Let's not "talk" so much about that, but decide to simply BE in this moment, by quietening our minds, opening our hearts, sitting peacefully in the stillness and calling God in to be present (whether our mate is physically available or not), in Divine Communion, with a sense of Oneness, in wholeness and completeness, with all of us right now.

CONFESSION #753 …

THE ONLY THING THAT MATTERS IS WHERE I AM RIGHT NOW

I'm not a failure, I'm just learning more. Nothing is wrong; in fact everything is going perfectly right. I don't hate my ex; I just got clearer about the relationship I really want. I'm not always disconnected; quite often I feel the fullness of "all that is". I don't have to focus on the worst; I can keep reaching for something so much better. I don't need to hold onto the things that cause pain; I can relax and allow things that bring relief instead. This situation doesn't need to cause me despair; I can activate the parts that thrill me beyond description. It's so much easier than I once thought.

CONFESSION #754 …

A NEW RELATIONSHIP IS FULL OF *FIRSTS*

With the excitement of getting to know one another for the first time, the thrill of first touch, first kiss, first body tingling sensation, first date, first heart thumping feelings, first uncertainty that I turn into certainty inside me and feel how powerful I am, first time we proudly hold hands in public, first time he finds out I'm not wearing underwear, first time he can't keep his eyes off me, first time we say I love you, first meeting with the family, first time we go shopping, first time we go jet skiing, first photo together, first time we announce we're a couple, first candlelight dinner, first picnic in the park, first time I feel him melt, first time I see him cry, first time I know exactly what to do, first Christmas, first gift that's so perfectly found, first intimate moment, first fondle of my breasts, first time he enters my body, first breakfast in bed, first holiday on a deserted island, first trip overseas, first time we wake up together, first time we walk on the beach, first time he gives me a surprise, first time he gives me another surprise, first time he asks me to be exclusive with him, first time I let him own my body and soul, first time we make plans together, first time we share a shower, first time I cry in his arms, first time I am a little chaotic and it turns him on madly, first time we lie naked on a bearskin rug in front of a roaring fire, first time we dance, first fight, first make-up, first time we realize we've gotten really close, first time we laugh until our stomachs hurt, first secret we share, first time we tell our deepest fantasies, first time he brings up the subject of marriage, first home together, first time we wrestle just for fun, first time we do something naughty in public, first time I do a slow and sensual striptease, first time I make him wait until we are both bursting to meld with each other, first time we do a new activity together, first time we play a game, first relationship strategy we share with others, first time he slowly licks the melted chocolate off my fingers, first time we say sorry, first time we spend hours just appreciating the memories we've made, what we have right now and the endless moments of firsts we'll enjoy for many more years into the future.

A LONG TERM RELATIONSHIP IS FULL OF *FIRSTS*

The first time we told a stranger about the most exciting thing we did together, the first time I stopped reminding him of his weakness and started talked about his strengths instead, first book of his positive aspects that I filled to the brim, first time I gave him what he's been asking for unconditionally, first time we decided to change the story we've been telling, first time we re-wrote our wedding vows to be the way we really wanted them, first time I stopped expecting our relationship to be perfect, first time we told the kids the naughty things we did, first time we spent hours talking about the great memories we've made, first time we shared a new sexual fantasy, the first time we stopped in the middle of harsh words and put a hand on each other's heart, the first time we pledged to be true to ourselves, the first time we allowed the other to break a rule without any consequences, the first time we decided to pretend that we were even more in love than ever … and then felt it happen.

CONFESSION #755 …

I TAKE RESPONSIBILITY FOR HOW I'M FEELING

When something upsets me, I have two basic choices:

1. To hate what's happening and make myself feel imprisoned by the circumstances OR

2. To find benefit in what's happening and set myself free.

It makes no difference what I think someone may have done to me they are never to blame for how I'm feeling; they aren't that powerful; unless I make them so.

CONFESSION #756 …

I DO WHAT I LOVE AND LOVE WHAT I DO

MAKING MONEY just takes the ability to follow a plan.

MAKING A HAPPY LIFE takes the commitment to follow my bliss.

Making money doesn't guarantee happiness but doing what I love to do tends to attract more money than I'll probably ever know what to do with. Don't you love knowing that?

CONFESSION #757 …

I'M INSPIRED TO NEW DESIRES

DESIRE … When I know what I don't want, which automatically causes me to know what I do want.

PAINFUL DESIRE … When I want something and I doubt it's even possible and berate myself for my inadequacies OR pretend I don't want it at all.

STRONG DESIRE … When I want something a whole lot and keep working hard trying to make it happen.

PURE DESIRE … When I want something and I expect it to come.

HEARTFELT DESIRE … When I want something with all my heart and I keep my mind deliberately tuned towards it as well.

CREATIVE DESIRE … When I want something, it feels good, I trust I'll be guided towards it and excitedly anticipate finding out how the universe will deliver it to me.

INSPIRED DESIRE … When I allow life to draw me towards the perfect contrasting experiences that take me quickly and directly to where I really want to go, allowing a new inspired desire to be born all over again.

CONFESSION #758 …

TODAY IS THE DAY THAT THINGS ARE GOING TO CHANGE

- and it's going to be fun
- and it's going to be good
- and it's going to be light
- and it's going to be joyful
- and it's going to be easy
- and it's going to be liberating
- and it's going to be guided
- and it's going to be just right!

CONFESSION #759 ...

I AM BESIDE MYSELF ... 😊

CONFESSION #760 …

I WAS BORN TO TREAT MYSELF WELL

Not try and prove how indestructible I am.

CONFESSION #761 …

TODAY IS GOING TO BE A GOOD DAY

I'm going to breathe deeper, speak less, think about how well I've done, be around people who make me laugh, appreciate the simple things, quieten my mind, look after myself better, trust the process, keep affirming that everything will work out, don't expect other people to understand and, "Hold My Hand On My Heart" before I say anything at all.

"Sometimes you have to pass through hell, before you realize what heaven really is."

CONFESSION #762 …

IT CAN HAPPEN IN A MOMENT

It only takes one moment to change a life one minute to make a mark, one instant to win a heart.

It only takes a new thought to change my state, one hope to set the scene, one wish to live the dream.

It only takes a helping hand to change another, one smile that cannot fail, an understanding word to lift the veil.

It only takes a fresh decision to start again, with a simple blessing from up above, granting a brand new life filled full of love.

CONFESSION #763 …

I CREATE THE ENVIRONMENT FOR SUCCESS

I measure success by how good I can make myself feel, so that in the midst of waiting for things to change I can still feel happy that it's on its way, I can still have faith that my questions have been answered, I can still believe that my solution has been created, I can relax in the knowing that what I want has already been given and I can feel total joy that the Universe has brought together all the components in the perfect timing, at the right place and in the most divine moment - right now.

> *"Feeling good is the most important manifestation of all."*

CONFESSION #764 …

I'M RELAXED ABOUT IT ALL

I'm so happy to know that what comes as a result of one experience is always so much better than the last. That when I have a problem, I can just relax and allow the solution. That when I ask a question, I can relax and allow the answer. That when I feel confusion, I can relax and allow the clarity. That when I want something to be different, I can relax and allow the change to occur. That when I need to find a new home, I can really relax and allow it to find me too.

CONFESSION #765 …

BIG PROBLEMS LEAD TO GREAT SOLUTIONS

Sometimes I love getting in such a predicament, that the only way it can possibly turn out well is if I give it to God to manage for all of us. Then I'm assured that it's set to turn out even better!

CONFESSION #766 ...

I DON'T TALK ABOUT MY PROBLEMS

This is Elizabeth.
Elizabeth is wise.

Although her life has its DOWNS like everyone else,
She just doesn't talk about her problems!

She prefers entertainment,
that lifts people UP! ... ☺

CONFESSION #767 …

I'M UPLIFTED

I LIFT MYSELF UP … I use meditation, walking on the beach, staying silent or being in solitude for a while (sometimes weeks on end) if I want to lift my vibe.

I DO IT GRADUALLY … I find it much more sustainable when I do it gradually. That's why people who take quantum leaps, have major awakenings and near death experiences can go through a type of depression for years afterwards; they know how amazing it is to feel "connected" and desperately want to get back there.

I DON'T RELY ON OTHER PEOPLE TO ASSIST - just the God Force I know IS me. Really sweet!

CONFESSION #768 ...

FEELING GOOD IS REALLY IMPORTANT TO ME

I LOVE IT WHEN I GET THAT FEELING ... that something is oh so right! That feeling of knowing, of absolute certainty, of complete and utter alignment with the path I'm choosing to take.

I LOVE IT WHEN I GET THAT FEELING ... of warm hearted love, from an openly inviting mind, with a sense of fluttering excitement, yet pervaded with a gentle stillness and to know that without a shadow of a doubt, everything is working, in Divine Timing and coming with such powerful clarity, that it will knock my socks off ... lol

CONFESSION #769 …

I HAVE THE POWER IN A RELATIONSHIP

But my power doesn't come from the ability to control my mate's behaviour! Real empowerment comes from knowing I can direct my focus and find things that make me happy, say things that draw a positive response, do things that feel like heaven, hold beliefs that stimulate soothing and have an attitude that makes me shine, no matter what my mate is up to.

CONFESSION #770 …

I'M SUCCESSFUL EVERY DAY

Success isn't something I achieve at the end of the journey. I feel incredibly successful each day as I relax my worries, tend to my happiness, do what I love to do and then watch as amazing opportunities are presented, tasks are done with a sense of delight and everything unfolds effortlessly along the way.

CONFESSION #771 …

NO MATTER WHAT YOU DO OR SAY, I LOVE YOU ANYWAY

My love for you doesn't depend on who you are, how you're behaving, what you look like, how wealthy you are or where you live. My love for you doesn't need you to be different, for some situation to improve or for you to even like me. I love you just because it feels good to love, it feels right to love and because love is who I am.

CONFESSION #772 …

SOMETIMES BEING POSITIVE JUST DOESN'T WORK

- when I'M trying too hard,
- when I'm wanting a particular result,
- when it just doesn't feel good anymore.

The whole purpose of being positive is because it makes me feel better! When it doesn't, then a good dose of anger or blame seems to do the trick … ☺ … then I can move on easily to feeling my empowered self again!

"I accept all my emotions, and let them pass easily, so I can spend more time feeling the ones I prefer."

CONFESSION #773 …

I'M CHOOSING AGAIN

I'm fully focused on my dreams and expanding on their magnetism, I'm looking towards my future and concentrating on its deliciousness, I'm letting go the worry about how I'm gonna make it happen and allowing it to unfold in vibrational perfection. I'm addicted to moving forward, to growing, to changing, to loving, to holding onto what feels good, to letting go what feels bad and to do whatever it takes to listen to the guidance pulsating from deep inside my soul.

CONFESSION #774 …

THERE'S NOTHING WRONG

I used to wonder if there was something wrong with me, when a mate left me for one reason or another. Now I realize there is actually something very *right* with me after all; because I can be happy, I'm meeting my own needs, I adore myself, I get variety, I'm finding excitement, I make life interesting, I still feel great passion, I always love deeply, whether I'm in a relationship or not.

CONFESSION #775 …

LOVE IS STRENGTH – LOVE IS ALIGNMENT

I USED TO THINK THAT LOVING YOU … meant that I should always give you what you were asking for. But that's not loving you, that's making you dependent on me for your happiness.

I LOVE YOU SO MUCH … that I won't let you manipulate me anymore. I won't allow you to keep thinking that controlling my behaviour will make you happy. True happiness is something you find inside yourself, and I love you so much that I'll keep on encouraging you to find your own alignment without relying on me or anyone else, to just roll over and give it to you.

But, if it feels right, if it comes from my heart, if it's bathed in the essence of real love, I'll give you more than you could have ever wished for.

CONFESSION #776 …

WANT TO ATTRACT A MAGNIFICENT RELATIONSHIP?

BE a person who appreciates the emotional growth, the spiritual connection and the deepest love that only physically intimate relationships can offer, and give it all you've got again and again and again … ☺

WANT TO CHOOSE A GREAT FEELING RELATIONSHIP?

Open to a man who's already "Satisfied" with what he's got. Find a woman who's totally "Happy" with Who She Is.

WANT TO STIMULATE MORE GOOD FEELINGS?

Make a woman feel really "Happy".
Make a man feel incredibly "Satisfied".

CONFESSION #777 …

THE UNIVERSE ADORES ME

Everything is working out beautifully. I don't have to know "how" the next phase will all happen, I don't have to sort it all out right now, I don't even need to have the perfect plan. I just remember to talk about what I want and why I want it.

I want to feel better, I want others to be happy, I want peace and understanding, I want life to be easier, I want even more adventure, I want to open my mind further, I want to expand my heart wider, I want to grow even wiser. I want to live, to love and to laugh with the most delirious passion I can possibly imagine.

CONFESSION #778 …

I'M PAMPERING MYSELF AS MUCH AS POSSIBLE

I'm hanging around people who are fun to be with, I'm taking more time out when something seems hard, I'm no longer assuming responsibility for how other people are feeling, I'm doing what seems right to me, I'm expecting wonderful things to happen, I'm deciding that life can be easy, I'm releasing myself from tending to the demands of others, I'm letting go all the stuff that hurts, I'm opening up to a more aligned relationship, I'm loving myself first and I'm living fully as if the Universe has the most incredible future in store for me.

CONFESSION #779 …

I'M GUIDED

But the guidance I receive doesn't always arrive with a chorus of angels, by the light of the silvery moon or carved in stone. Most times the messages are subtle, like a sigh of relief, a spontaneous smile, a warm sensation in my heart, a tingle on my tongue and a lightening of the load - as if my creator has already found what I am reaching for and is calling me home.

CONFESSION #780 ...

I CAN FEEL GOOD RIGHT NOW

I CARE "MORE" ABOUT THIS MOMENT ... than about what happened yesterday. I care that I make the most of what I have, not complain about what I'm missing. I care that I feel good about everything I do, not do things just out of obligation.

HOW I FEEL MATTERS ... what I give my attention to matters, what I believe is possible for my future matters and what I'm focusing on right now is to allow myself to have more fun, to feel more joy, to notice more beauty, to experience more peace, to gain more understanding and to share more love than ever before ... I can feel that, right now in this moment, can you?

CONFESSION #781 ...

I HAVE AN EFFECTIVE WAY OF UPLIFTING A RELATIONSHIP

- When someone's not behaving well - don't mention it.
- When someone's in a bad mood - don't mention it.
- When someone's disconnected from "who they really are" - don't mention it.
- When someone's felt the need to complain - don't mention it.
- When someone's been really angry, depressed or negative - don't mention it.
- When someone's done something that hurts me - don't mention it.

We all know when we're not being our best. I've developed such a security about Who I Am that I don't need someone else to change so I can feel better.

- I can stop taking things so personally,
- I can let go of the past,
- I can live in the way that's right for me and
- I CAN LEAD BY EXAMPLE and show them how it's done.

CONFESSION #782 …

I THRIVE IN ALL CONDITIONS

Relationship challenges are always temporary and only last as long as I keep thinking about them. So I go out and have as much fun as I can and don't let them affect me, or else I'd get caught up in the drama of it all and be no use to anyone.

A relationship can still thrive, even if one mate is temporally facing challenges, even if one mate seems to be temporally heading in a different direction, even if one mate is temporarily seeing someone else, even if one mate is temporarily missing in action.

One person who's aligned with love can positively influence the lives of many and profoundly shape the course of the future.

CONFESSION #783 …

I LIVE A LIFE OF LUXURY

I once thought that luxury meant buying something expensive! Then I realized it doesn't cost much, to take time out and free my mind, to turn myself on and thrill my senses, to make a fabulous home cooked meal and tantalize my taste buds, to soak in a hot bath and relax my body, to think of someone I adore and warm my heart; to me, they're greater luxuries than money can ever buy. As I'm in the business of Creating Wealth for myself and others, I remind myself that the goal isn't *success*; the real goal is the happiness I think the success will bring.

CONFESSION #784 …

TODAY I ASKED FOR A MIRACLE

I imagined the end result with excitement of what was possible. I found appreciation for the situation that had called for an improved solution. I felt the peacefulness of faith in the benevolence of this amazing Universe. I sensed the calmness of knowing as I expected it to come. In perfect timing, in Divine synchronicity, in communion with others and in better ways that even I could have dreamed up alone.

CONFESSION #785 …

SOMETIMES I FEEL TERRIBLE AND I WANT TO FEEL BETTER

When I feel like crap and nothing else is working, posting photos on Facebook of cute animals sometimes helps.

When I feel like crap and nothing else is working, saying something really ridiculous usually make me laugh. I find humor is one of the best ways to change anything.

When I feel like crap and nothing else is working, I decide how I want to feel instead. I don't aim to change my mood instantly, but remember that I can more easily feel better, bit by bit.

When I feel like crap and I want to feel better, letting myself get REALLY angry and then having a good cry sometimes helps, yep, that feels a bit better already.

When I feel like crap and I want to feel better, accepting that "I am where I am" and asking others to just let me be, is a really good place to start. Making peace with where I'm at has a unique way of allowing the next action to be inspired instead of trying to "force" the energy to shift.

When I feel like crap and I want to feel better, I do whatever I can to distract myself from my worries, have a chat with some supportive imaginary friends, take time away from the person who's been bothering me or meditate on my navel, because my navel loves me just the way I am … ☺

When I feel like crap and I want to feel better, taking the time to talk with some friendly animals always gives me a lift.

When I feel like crap and I want to feel better, I remind myself that sometimes it's OK to play in the "real world". Then I do whatever it takes to get back to fantasyland again, where happiness, bliss and euphoria abound, everything I desire is created in my imagination and sooner or later ALL my dreams come true.

When someone else feels like crap, I remind myself that they'll find their own way through, without trying to fix them, or change them, or tell them what I think they should do. There's nothing more annoying to someone who's feeling bad, than having someone tell them they should be doing something different. While I might appreciate my clarity of mind, it may be appropriate for someone else to be growing through confusion.

When someone else feels like crap and I want them to feel better, remembering how amazing they really are (no matter what momentary phase they're going through) is the best thing I can ever do for them.

When someone else feels like crap, trying to change them is an indication I'm NOT accepting my own imperfections … Allowing them to just BE and remembering who they really are inside, is an indication that I'm trusting the process of life to naturally guide us back towards the light, towards our own truth and towards being again the incredibly loving person who lives in the heart of each one of us.

CONFESSION #786 ...

I DON'T NEED TO GET RID OF "NEGATIVE" PEOPLE

This is Elizabeth.
Elizabeth is really smart.
She never needs to get rid of negative people from her life or she'd be being negative just like them.
Be really smart like Elizabeth.
Look at them so lovingly
they just can't think of anything negative to say ... ♡

CONFESSION #787 …

I'M SECURE

I didn't look for someone who'll promise to love me so I can feel safe. I'm determined to love myself so much, that it makes no difference whether they're having a low moment or feel on top of the world. That type of emotional security lasts a lifetime!

CONFESSION #788 …

I LOVE RELATIONSHIPS

I love waking up in my man's arms. Rolling over and smiling as his eyes meet mine. I love placing my hand on his knee as we drive and to feel him squeeze it in appreciation. I love the way he reaches for my hand as we walk down the street, how he watches out for me when we're in a crowded room, how he always looks after me as I walk off into the sunset (or into the next shop ... lol). I love how he stimulates my juices, makes my heart thump faster and just takes my breath away when he stares intimately into the deepest part of my soul.

CONFESSION #789 …

I CAN CHANGE DIRECTION RIGHT NOW

It doesn't matter what happened before, right now is when I can turn it all around, right now is when I can change my focus, right now is when I can remember the wholeness that IS me, right now is why the future will be even more blissfully Divine.

CONFESSION #790 …

THE UNIVERSE IS ALWAYS WORKING FOR ME

To give me answers to my most puzzling questions, to create solutions for my most pressing problems, to bring me everything I've ever asked for in even better ways than I can imagine. I just remind myself to relax and have faith that what I want has already been given, and it was given before I even asked!

CONFESSION #791 …

I ATTRACT THE LOVE I GIVE TO MYSELF

When I pay attention to loving myself first, it becomes irrelevant what other people think of me. My happy, carefree and naturally loving nature always attracts the most amazing opportunities, wonderful people and delightfully respectful mates, just like bees are attracted to pollen.

CONFESSION #792 …

I'M ENJOYING THE RIDE

The greatest excitement I get in life, is when I reach for something I don't know for sure I can have. Getting the goal is an anti-climax, but the intoxicating thrill of stepping just outside my comfort zone, is what makes the ride worthwhile.

CONFESSION #793 …

I KEEP MY HEART AND MIND WIDE OPEN

The only thing that has ever hurt me emotionally was when I opened my heart, expected something in return and then closed my heart again. In relationships, we often try to enforce fidelity, we want them to last forever, and we expect our mate to put US first. In life we often demand certain behaviour, we only want to make friends with those who agree with us and we judge whether someone is right or wrong. BUT, the more that we ask other people to be different, the further we get from expressing, experiencing and BEING who we really are! Naturally, unconditionally, loving at our core.

CONFESSION #794 …

I HAVE THE FINEST QUALITIES

My soul-mate didn't come through a list of criteria I wanted in him. My soul mate was born from the qualities I cultivated in myself.

CONFESSION #795 …

I NEVER GET JEALOUS

Jealousy is only possible when I expect something in return for the love I've given. Instead, I choose to love unconditionally, then it's impossible to be hurt (because I only give what I want to give), it's impossible to lose (because I wasn't expecting a particular result), it's impossible to get jealous, (because I ONLY do what feels right for me) and want my mate to be true to himself too; not to some outdated commitment that takes away our freedom to choose what's right for us in any given moment.

CONFESSION #796...

IT COMES EVERY TIME

Whenever I ask a question, the answer is always given. I just need to be in a more relaxed or receiving or trusting or hopeful or happy mode in order to hear it. There is NO limit to the ways an answer can be received. I just allow it to come in the best way it can ... and it does, every time.

CONFESSION #797…

THERE'S POWER IN ALIGNMENT

I've never needed to get others to agree with me, to sign petitions, to join groups that are for or against something. I know that when I am attuned to the love and light that IS me, I am far more influential that a herd of people who are trying to gain more power with numbers or fight for their rights by making someone else wrong. Quiet, peaceful and personal alignment creates more transformational momentum than a surge of protesters can possibly produce.

CONFESSION #798…

I'M IN LOVE

I'm in love in such a beautiful kind of way.
I don't expect that love give me something in return, I don't expect that love be faithful,
I don't expect perfection or honest communication, I don't expect it to work,
I don't expect it to last, I don't even care if love likes me at all. I just enjoy the feeling of sharing the love, expanding the love, talking about love and BEING the love, that inside is the essence of me.

> *"Love isn't just what you find in someone else, it's what you dare to allow yourself to become."*

CONFESSION #799…

I'VE BEEN BLESSED

I've been blessed with the gift of being able to see the beauty, the magnificence, the perfection in everyone. I never treat celebrities, wealthy people or gurus like they're more important than anyone else! Being put on a pedestal always feels a little "off", but, acknowledging the positive aspects of each person I meet and making them feel special in their own right, is one of the most fulfilling and heart-warming things I've ever done.

CONFESSION #800 …

I MADE DECISIONS THAT CHANGED MY LIFE

I decided that things could be easier, so I RELAXED a little more. I decided I wanted more love in my life, so I GAVE a little more. I decided today is the perfect time, to change my point of view, and to appreciate what I have right now as if it's all brand new.

I realized there were things that I wanted, that I believed I just couldn't have. Then I assumed I shouldn't want them, 'cause it made me feel really bad. But wanting them wasn't the problem, into my heart they'd already been thrust, so I found the faith to remember, all I need to do is trust.

So I decided to trust my feelings, and let them guide me through the day, I decided that if something feels good to me, if it calls me out to play … if it lights up my life and opens my mind, there's nothing more I need from above, my bright energy attracts everything I could possibly want, my heart leads me back to love.

But sometimes I just don't feel any good, and it seems nothing I do or say, can find the connection I once enjoyed, peace seems oh so far away. It's times like these I need to chill out, to let go, to do my best, and hand it over to "The Universe" to fix up all the rest.

In this moment I'd like to affirm, that there IS something I can do, to make my days go better and to uplift someone else's too. I can decide to make peace with whatever's happening, to find the heaven contained in hell, no matter what seems to be going wrong, we are still loved and "All Is Well".

CONFESSION #801 …

I'M EMOTIONAL

My emotions go up and down, just like the passionate, fascinating, deliciously sensual, vivacious woman I'm meant to be. I throw myself into life, not pussyfoot around trying to always achieve balance. I'm real with how I feel in the moment and no longer cover it up in an attempt to achieve some sort of perfection. I'm reveling in those parts of me that I was once too scared to show and have decided to make what anyone else might think about it, completely, utterly and totally irrelevant.

"I'm so proud of me!"

CONFESSION #802 …

I CAN GET WHAT I WANT

But first, I have to let go thinking that it should happen in a particular way. When I ask for something, it's always given, but I can only see if, hear it, feel it, taste it and touch it, when I stop resisting, and ALLOW it to come, in the best way it can.

CONFESSION #803 ...

I DON'T GIVE OTHER PEOPLE ADVICE

This is Elizabeth.
Elizabeth once thought she was smart.
So she used to give people advice on Facebook just to show everyone else how smart she was too.
Then she decided to take her own advice, looked in the mirror and quickly realized, that if she really was THAT smart she would have drawn herself with a short skirt, long eyelashes, shapely legs, and really sexy shoes ... ☺

CONFESSION #804 …

I AM ENCOURAGING

My job as a coach, mentor or parent is not to give the best advice based on my past experience, my fears for their future, my extensive training or some extremely compelling research. My job is simply to encourage them into that empowering "state of confidence" which helps them access more clearly their own sense of knowing what is right or wrong for them.

"Instead of fostering dependency, I prefer to encourage self-sufficiency".

CONFESSION #805 …

I DON'T HELP ANYONE

I show them how to help themselves.

My main intention is to uplift myself and let those who feel good being around me, naturally find their own benefit. There's nothing more inspiring than leading by example.

Whenever I tried to help other people because I thought they needed it, my work seemed to have minimal effect (and it was often hard). Whenever I started with an intention to uplift myself, other people naturally found their own benefits, and my work became a total joy (and it was effortless too). I reconnected to my own powerful knowing that tending to my attitude and focusing on my own inner growth is by far the BEST way to lead anyone.

> *"A different intention produces vastly different results."*

CONFESSION #806 …

I DON'T WORK ON MY PROBLEMS

I find it so much more productive to just acknowledge the issue AND then use it to define what I want and where I prefer to go, rather than focus on where I've been and what I should be letting go. One keeps me anchored in the troubles of the past. The other moves me forward rapidly to the future of my dreams.

CONFESSION #807 …

IT'S NOT MY JOB TO LOVE OTHERS

I once thought that my purpose was to love other people. But you know what? Sometimes I've been such a problem to them, that it harassed them into loving themselves. And that's even better!

CONFESSION #808 ...

I REVEALED THE 7 BIGGEST MYTHS

MYTH #1 ... WHEN YOU HAVE A GOOD HEART, YOU GET HURT

You don't get hurt because you have a good heart. You got hurt because you ignored your inner guidance, over and over and over again. When something feels off - it IS off!

MYTH #2 ... REALITY IS HARSH

REALITY is only harsh because you're giving IT more attention than your dreams.

MYTH #3 ... I CAN'T GET WHAT I WANT BECAUSE OTHERS ARE INVOLVED

Your dreams are pure. When you pay too much attention to what you think other people are wanting, you lose sight of what's possible for you to create. But, when you stay gently focused on your dreams, doors open, pathways unfold, opportunities present themselves that you otherwise might not have imagined possible.

MYTH #4 ... LIFE IS TEACHING US A LESSON

Not True. LIFE is simply reflecting back to us, what our dominant thoughts and emotions have been. Change the dominant thoughts and emotions and change the conditions of your life.

MYTH #5 ... MY FEELINGS GET ME IN TROUBLE

That only happens when you doubt them, when you keep digging deeper to find more proof of what you already instinctively know or when you make yourself wrong for having them in the first place. All feelings are guidance, moving you further from or bringing you closer to, what you really want for your life. That is all.

MYTH #6 … IT TAKES TWO

Not True. I once believed that "it takes two to make a relationship work", but each time I said it, I was giving my power to the other person. Then …

- I decided to take responsibility for how

I feel, totally.
- I let my mate off the hook, completely.
- I thought about funny stuff that made me laugh, deliberately.
- I talked of all sorts of things that made me happy, joyfully

... and I found out really quickly that it doesn't need two, it just needs ME, to show up as the incredible person I always knew myself to be. "I'm a leader and I'm ready to shine!"

MYTH #7 ... I HAVE TO WORK HARD TO MAKE A LIVING

False. You don't even have to work at all, to have things come to you. (Remember those good things that've come seemingly out of the blue?) Just DON'T contradict what you want with doubt, with negative conversations, with trying too hard to achieve a result, with getting other people to approve, with thinking you have to do it all by yourself.

Have you noticed, that when you're off having a good time, or you fall in love, or you're involved in a task that brings you tremendous pleasure, the rest of your life tends to balance out too?

That's why sex, orgasm and masturbation work so well. They take us momentarily out of our resistant minds and connect us more fully to spirit. But aligning the body, mind AND spirit is what makes anything more sustainable.

CONFESSION #809 …

I LOVE FEELING GOOD

If something feels good, I do it over and over again, with no judgment, rules or evaluation about what's appropriate and what isn't. But if there's some sort of guilt attached to it, I stop immediately, because my intention is always to feel as wonderful as I can, and guilt is the clear indication I'm going backwards.

CONFESSION #810 ...

I ACCEPT ALL MY EMOTIONS

- I can feel powerless and use it as a springboard to change.
- I can allow depression to run its course.
- I can use anger to get relief.
- I can understand the process of revenge.
- I can explore blame.
- I can openly express negativity or doubt.
- I can find stillness through boredom.
- I can get encouraged by hope.
- I can start to feel more optimistic again.
- I can find enthusiasm when I think about what's possible.
- I can choose to believe things are getting better and better.
- I can expect good things to happen.
- I can align my intentions with fun and happiness and joy.
- I can relax into a state of calm and bliss.
- I can surge into ecstasy.
- I can powerfully escalate my level of appreciation.
- I can resonate fully into total oneness with all of life.

CONFESSION #811 …

I'M ENJOYING AN UNCONDITIONALLY LOVING RELATIONSHIP

It's up to me to give what I want, when I want, with whoever I want, at any time I want and to follow my bliss as I do it. I don't need my mate to agree, to make a commitment, to promise me anything at all. I just want him to do what's right for him in any given moment.

INTEGRITY can't be written into a vow based on my experiences from the past in a hope the future will be assured. It can only be lived by fully embracing, the newness of the present.

CONFESSION #812 …

I FEEL THE LOVE AND EXPRESS IT

Love is not about what someone else is giving me; it's always about where I'm at. I say "I LOVE YOU" in any moment I feel it, to strangers, to my lover, to my kids, to my pets, to a piece of art, to music that moves me, to my dishwasher (the electric one and the manual one …☺), to myself and to the safe and inviting home that I create wherever I am in the world.

CONFESSION #813 …

MORE GOOD STUFF KEEPS COMING

When I focus on all the wonderful things I already have in my life, the other things I'd like to have as well, just seem to show up to fill in the gaps.

CONFESSION #814 ...

I DON'T GET DISSAPPOINTED

Instead, I've increased my Faith.

When I stopped trying to control the people around me by expecting them to behave in a certain way, I automatically started to trust that The Universe/God might handle things even better than I could alone. Now I'm surprised and delighted beyond comprehension almost every single day.

CONFESSION #815 …

I'M FOLLOWING MY DREAM

I know what I want. I know it's already mine. I'm making space for it to show up. I'm going in the right direction. I'm loving the ride. I've got even more incredible adventures to look forward to. I want to find more and more ways to express my greatest passions. I'm ready. It's here. I can relax and just let it in.

CONFESSION #816 ...

BEING COMMITTED WORKS FOR ME

This is Elizabeth

Elizabeth has so much freedom
that sometimes she likes to imagine ...

... being tied down in a relationship ... ☺

CONFESSION #817 …

YOU DON'T NEED TO CHANGE

Come just as you are, and it's my intention that we'll both part feeling even better than when you arrived.

CONFESSION #818 …

4 STRATEGIES THAT BOOST THE ENERGY IN MY RELATIONSHIP.

1. I TAKE CARE OF MY OWN NEEDS FIRST. When I'm full of love for life; the people around me are showered with affection, appreciation and praise. I need nothing from them and can give from a totally unconditional place.

    "We only NEED something from others when we haven't been looking after ourselves."

2. I TREAT MYSELF WELL. After reading "Men Are from Mars Women Are From Venus", I started practicing BEING OK when a guy takes time out from the relationship (also called "going to his cave"). I make sure I nurture my body, mind and soul beautifully while he's temporarily absent and TRUST he would come back even stronger than before.

3. I OPEN MY HEART BEFORE I OPEN MY MOUTH. After working extensively with the teachings of Abraham Hicks, I now do whatever it takes to get myself into my happy/empowered/centered place BEFORE I have an important conversation with my mate, before sex, before we go out, before I do almost anything at all.

4. I'M HONEST HOW I'M REALLY FEELING. After many wonderful relationships I've found there's nothing that moves energy quicker than being honest and open about where I'm at emotionally, BUT always with an intention to clear the air, to help myself feel better and NOT make my mate responsible for any of it.

CONFESSION #819 …

I PUT MYSELF FIRST

As soon as I start to feel anxious or resentful, it's my signal to take care of my own needs immediately, without judgment, without expecting myself to be perfect all the time and to do whatever it takes to LOVE MYSELF UNCONDITIONALLY FIRST.

"It all starts with me."

CONFESSION #820 …

I MAKE LIFE EASY

It doesn't matter what happens, I thrive through adversity and I expand even more in the presence of great love. I once thought that creating drama was the most exciting way to survive, now I know that gentle transformation is not only more sustainable, but in pure alignment with the way my life was meant to be lived.

*"Notice what I don't want.
Focus on what I do want.
So easy!"*

CONFESSION #821 …

IT FEELS GOOD TO LOVE

I love you. Not because you did anything special, not because we have many things in common, not because I want something in return and not even because I should!

"I love you just because LOVING feels so incredibly good!"

CONFESSION #822 …

I LOVE BEING IN A RELATIONSHIP

For me, there's one compelling reason to be in a relationship. It's not so I can feel loved, it's not so I can be supported, it's not so I can share responsibilities, it's simply to enjoy what I've already got, who I already am and where I intend to take my life, with another incredible person.

CONFESSION #823…

I'VE FOUND A WAY TO APPRECIATE EVERYTHING

I choose how I respond to everything that happens.

- If I DON'T like what's showing up, I appreciate it for helping me re-define my path.
- If I DO like what's showing up I appreciate it for giving me what I've asked for.

Either way I get to appreciate EVERYTHING.

CONFESSION #824 ...

I LET PEOPLE KNOW I APPRECIATE THEM

This is Elizabeth.
Elizabeth is wise.
She doesn't wait for birthdays, special occasions or funerals to let people know how much she loves and appreciates them.
She likes to love and appreciate people EVERY day.
Be wise like Elizabeth
and spend lots of time acknowledging the things that warm your heart too.
She sure LOVES and APPRECIATES you.

CONFESSION #825 …

HOPE IS GOOD

I only need to hope for something and within minutes I can find evidence that it's on its way to me. But the most profound miracles tend to occur inside ME first, setting forth a bold new inspiration, suggesting a gently altered perception, instilling a feeling of ease and trust.

> *"Good things flow naturally when I open my eyes, my mind and my heart and just let them in."*

CONFESSION #826 ...

I MEET MY OWN NEEDS

I don't expect anyone in particular to meet my needs. Not my mate, not my kids, not my friends and not even the government. If there's something I want, I just relax and allow it to come through the path of least resistance.

"Life can be so easy, when I just let it be ... ☺
"

CONFESSION #827 …

I DIDN'T FIND SUCCESS BY LOOKING FOR IT

I claimed success by being true to myself, by being true to my needs, by being true to what I wanted and by letting the good things in life match up to my truth.

CONFESSION #828 …

I FEEL YOU IN MY HEART

I sense your presence in my dreams, I've made space for you to be here by my side, I smell your scent on the breeze, I feel a deep sense of comfort when I think of you wanting to be with me too and I know instinctively that you're so close, that I keep expecting to bump into you at any minute - and feel the relief of knowing, you were certainly worth waiting for!

"Lying next to you is like melting into liquid love."

CONFESSION #829 …

I HAVE PREFERENCES

I would rather listen to music than read the news, I would rather play than be serious, I would rather speak from the heart than speak my mind, I would rather drink water than wine, I would rather hear stories about an intriguing future than about the issues from the past and I would much rather be with you, than anywhere else on earth.
But most of all, I prefer to feel in alignment with Source right now, without needing to change anything at all.

CONFESSION #830 …

I DO IT ALL TO MYSELF

Love doesn't hurt, but withholding my love sure does.

CONFESSION #831 …

I PAY ATTENTION TO WHAT I LIKE

I might notice your faults, but I don't give them any attention at all. I prefer to spend my time wisely and concentrate on the type of behaviour that I want to encourage.

CONFESSION #832 …

I'M THOUGHTFUL ABOUT THE STORY I TELL

The way I talk about my life experiences either takes me further away or bring me closer to where I really want to go. If the story I'm telling makes me feel worse, I don't tell it at all. If the story I'm telling makes me feel better, I shout it from the rooftops.

CONFESSION #833 ...

I USE COMMUNICATION STRATEGIES

If I'm ever bothered by what people are saying, I have these empowered options to choose from:

- As they're talking I can imagine what they might really be wanting underneath all the bull-dust.
- I can use it to determine what I really want instead.
- I can practice my skills to accept another point of view without trying to change it.
- I can maintain my own state of "Presence" with full knowing of who We Both Really Are.
- I can ignore them completely and let the energy dissipate.
- I can change the subject.
- I can find clever or really funny ways to break their pattern.
- I can excuse myself and take space away from them until I compose myself again.
- I can block them from contacting me.

No one ever needs to step in and protect me.

I take complete responsibility for what I allow into my life. I don't need other people's agreement that someone else is behaving badly nor do I need approval for the actions I choose to take, other than "It Feels Right For Me".

The more I step in to protect others, the less they get to learn to follow their own guidance and empower themselves.

The more I demonstrate useful life skills, the easier it is to see that "anything can be taken as a compliment.

CONFESSION #834 …

I'M SOLUTION ORIENTATED

Whenever there's a problem I can search for the cause of the problem, and try to get to the bottom of it.

OR

I can find things that make me feel better that open my mind, that expand my heart, that uplift my spirits and help everyone else around me feel better as well. That's the solution we were seeking all along.

CONFESSION #835 …

THE BEST STRATEGY OF ALL

To just be myself! Without worrying about what other people might think, without needing their approval or permission, without wanting to please them, without feeling constricted by rules and regulations, without trying to hide my real feelings, without being afraid of what I might lose and by giving complete and utter attention to what I have to gain instead.

CONFESSION #836 …

EVERYTHING'S GOING MY WAY

Not just because I live in one of the most magnificent places on the planet, not just because I've been given so many incredible gifts and not just because my heart is fully open, everything goes my way because I DECIDED it is.

CONFESSION #837 ...

I ONCE WANTED WORLD PEACE

But when I really thought about it, I would have been condemning someone else's choices in order to get it. That's not real peace, that's conditional righteousness. Now I prefer to claim the "Peace in My Heart" which is an inner journey, and one that I choose to take privately, as often as I can. From there, Miracles happen!

CONFESSION #838 ...

I LET GO

When things happen quickly I stop holding onto how I think my life should be and decide to *Let Go* and just *Enjoy The Ride*.

CONFESSION #839 …

I STOPPED

It's such a relief to decide that I actually don't have to work harder to reach some "perfect" standard. What I really need to do is just stop condemning my "imperfections".

CONFESSION #840 …

THE PAST IS IRRELEVANT

While most people want to know as much as they can about a potential mate, a new friend, a boss or a co-worker, I prefer to be told as little as possible. I want my imagination, my beliefs and my vision to draw out their inner essence right now, in the perfection of this very moment.

"Leave the past on the past and look eagerly forward, to what we have the potential to create tomorrow."

CONFESSION #841 …

I'M IMPRESSED

This is Elizabeth.
Elizabeth is clever.
She doesn't post pictures of herself with just any old guru, celebrity, musician or actor to try to impress you and get you to like her more.

Be clever like Elizabeth.
Go straight to the top …

… and Photoshop yourself in with God … ☺

CONFESSION #842 …

THE POWER IS IN YOUR HEART

You don't need ME to love YOU. But you can feel my love in any moment that you stop what you're doing, put your hand on your heart, take the deepest breath and be open to receive, just like that!

CONFESSION #843 …

I'M A GIVER

I've never felt the need to FIND the greatest love of my life. I just have the overwhelming desire to GIVE the greatest love to someone else.

CONFESSION #844 …

WHEN IT'S RIGHT – YOU KNOW IT!

There are no words to explain just how *right* something can feel.

CONFESSION #845 …

I CHANGE MY BELIEFS

A belief is just a thought I keep thinking, just a view I keep expressing, just a story that either takes me to a better place or keeps me stuck, right where I am. I can change my beliefs as often as I change my clothes, in order to keep me pointing with decisive intent, towards what I really want for my life.

"I always have, I still do and I believe I always will, think we are totally AMAZING!"

CONFESSION #846 …

I HAVE GREAT FAITH

Faith can make the impossible, possible!

Faith is when I hold a vision of what I want with such certainty, that it MUST "be"! My vision doesn't need to include faces and places, details and steps. Most times, it's better if it doesn't. The important ingredient has always been to choose the "feelings" it will contain and then cause myself to know them so completely, that life can do nothing else but bring the physical elements towards me with such intensity, we merge into each other.

CONFESSION #847 …

I MAKE EXCELLENT CHOICES

I CHOOSE MORE CLEARLY with my feelings, not my words.

I CHOOSE MORE POWERFULLY when I'm in the fullness of my heart, not when I'm reacting in my mind.

I CHOOSE MORE SUSTAINABLY when I'm open to a solution, not when I'm trying to prevent a problem.

I CHOOSE MORE WISELY when I relax into the contrast, when I bless the events that brought me here, when I'm actively appreciating what I've already been given and when I'm keenly looking forward to the goodness, that's still to come.

> "I CHOOSE to thrive in all situations, against all odds and in all ways."

CONFESSION #848 …

NOTHING IS RIGHT OR WRONG

I do anything it takes to uplift my spirits, with NO judgment about what's appropriate, with NO doubt about what makes me feel better, with NO concern about whether it's sustainable, with no fear about the potential consequences. When I feel better, any past problems turn into immediate solutions, any issues just stop making sense at all and anybody around me feels so much better as well.

CONFESSION #849 …

I CHANGED MY ATTITUDE ABOUT MEN

When I changed my attitude about men, what I attracted changed dramatically too!

- I love men
- I love the clarity they offer to dating and relationships
- I love their sex drive - for without it we probably wouldn't get together at all
- I love giving them opportunities to please me, warm me, relax with me and melt into me
- I love being so sure of who I am that THEY can stuff up and know I'll ignore it completely
- I love drawing out their positive aspects by using the power of MY focus
- I love making myself so happy that I don't need them to behave in any particular way at all
- I love being able to tease them sexually, playfully, whimsically and soulfully - oh my God, and they love it too
- I love being able to lead with my heart, so they can do the hard yards and create with

- their minds
- I love knowing that at their core they want to protect, to cherish, to adore and to value me highly
- I love the balance they add to my "sometimes" erratic feminine energy … lol
- I love that they openly appreciate who I am
- I love their willingness to lead, and drive the car, and follow their mission and live with purpose - that inspires me to raise my power as well
- I love how they appreciate my "positive" encouragement and hope it never comes across as belittling their incredible natural skills
- I love the many times I've been given second chances to be truly understood
- I love that they don't let women dictate HOW they should behave
- I love that they stand firm in the face of silly feminine criticism
- I love, value and deeply appreciate their presence on this planet

"… and, I APPRECIATE the special man in my life, more than words can say."

CONFESSION #850 …

I HAVE A LIFE OF TOTAL FREEDOM

Not because I was born rich, not because I worked hard and earned it, not because I got lucky and not even because I made great business decisions.

I have a life of total freedom because I consistently held the belief that "I can have whatever I want" without needing to justify why I want it, without needing to feel guilty about it, without needing to prove how smart, good or worthy I am and without needing to follow the crowd. I allow an avalanche of wonderful things to flow to me because life is created by what I BELIEVE it can be!

And I STOPPED diluting my beliefs by trying to get anyone else to agree with me, by seeking advice from some guru or by listening to the stupid opinions of others. I stand firm in what I know to be true. "I AM The Creator of the Life That's Just Right for Me!"

*"I have a life of total freedom
just because I wanted it, I asked for it
and I expected it to be."*

CONFESSION #851 …

I'M A CREATOR

STRUGGLE IS ... when you assume the big pleasures of life are harder to obtain than the simple ones.

CREATING IS ... when you relax and allow the big pleasures to unfold as easily and naturally, as you expect the simple ones to do.

CONFESSION #852 …

NOTHING REALLY MATTERS

When I'm enjoying moving my body, it doesn't really matter who I'm dancing with.

When I'm loving who I am as a person, it doesn't really matter who I have a relationship with.

When I'm noticing the scent in the air, the songs of the birds, the gentleness of the breeze, it doesn't really matter what the blinkin' weather is doing.

When I'm appreciating my day being just as it is, it doesn't really matter how much money I'm making, where I am, who I'm with, or what's happening in my life, I'm as high as a kite and the entire world looks beautiful … ☺

CONFESSION #853 …

THERE ARE TWO WAYS TO COMMUNICATE

1. Am I attempting to expose someone's weakness?

    OR

2. Am I inspired to draw out their strengths?

"Either way, my prime motivation can clearly be seen reflected in the result."

CONFESSION #854 …

I CAN DO THIS

It only takes one of us to shift the energy in a conflict from discomfort to ease, from judgment to acceptance, from annoyance to harmony. I can do it without needing the other persons agreement, without them being involved, without them even knowing.

By making peace with my THOUGHTS, by gently moving my own FEELINGS from anger to hope, by engaging in CONVERSATIONS that are uplifting and most often, by simply being still in the silence and handing it all over to God.

CONFESSION #855 ...

I DON'T ALWAYS BELIEVE YOU

I only choose to believe things that uplift, enhance, expand and liberate both of us.

CONFESSION #856 …

I PLAY GAMES

When I think someone else is to blame, it's always my attitude that's in need of a change. So I dust myself off and play a new game.

- STOP focusing on the negatives … build from the positives.
- STOP talking about their shortcomings … remember their magnificence.
- STOP thinking that "they" are the problem … know that "I" am the solution.
- STOP reacting to their smallness … demonstrate my greatness.
- STOP concentrating on the bad times … remind them of the good ones.
- STOP withholding what they're wanting … give it unconditionally.
- STOP expecting the worst … imagine the best.
- STOP wanting them to change … change my perspective, my attitude or my proximity to the problem.
- STOP fighting for my rights … find peace in my heart and be the leader I was always meant to be.

CONFESSION #857 ...

I DON'T NEED TO IMPRESS YOU

This is Elizabeth.
Elizabeth is wise.

Today she went out for a drive with Bill.

Elizabeth thinks that it's a good idea to post a random picture of your day out on Facebook, but next time you do it, be wise like Elizabeth,

and DON'T TAG Shelli and 49 others,

because people get annoyed with it ...

... and no one really gives a duck ... ☺

CONFESSION #858 ...

I LIKE CONTRAST

I like contrast telling me that something's a bit off.

- I like THE CLARITY that it provides.
- I like DECIDING what I want instead.
- I like TRUSTING my feelings to show me how to get there.
- I like FOCUSING in a more positive direction - happily.
- I like IMAGINING what it will be like - vividly.
- I like FINDING my own equilibrium - peacefully.
- I like OPENING my heart and mind to solutions - faithfully.
- I like KNOWING things will sort themselves out - perfectly.
- I like EXPANDING into new places.
- I like BELIEVING I can have it all.
- I like REMEMBERING all the times things have worked out before.
- I like APPRECIATING what I've got right now.

- I like CREATING the vibe for stuff I want to manifest
- I like LOVING it into being.
- I like MOMENTUM growing - steadily.
- I like FLOWING - freely.
- I like ALLOWING all sorts of wonderful things to come to me - easily
- I like BEING the designer of my life.

CONFESSION #859 …

I FIND THE POSITIVE INTENT

I find comfort in seeking out the positive intention behind other people's behavior. Whenever I'm wanting to turn an uncomfortable conversation into an understanding one, I ask myself, "What is this person really intending underneath everything? Is it to protect, to prevent, to produce or to provide something?"

Asking this one simple question over and over has restored, transformed and significantly enhanced several of the most important relationships in my life.

"At the foundation of every behaviour is a positive intent".

CONFESSION #860 …

I'M LOW MAINTENANCE

When I realized I could have anything I wanted, I found out I hardly needed anything at all.

CONFESSION #861 …

I'M IN HEAVEN

It feels like heaven, it feels like ease, it feels like luxury, it feels like perfection, it feels like it was always meant to be, it feels like floating, it feels like stability, it feels like certainty, it feels like peace, it feels like gentle harmony, it feels like softness, it feels like cooperation, it feels like tingling, it feels like warmth, it feels like comforting arms have always been wrapped gently around me, it feels like the most natural thing in the world.

CONFESSION #862 …

I'M LOVED FOR WHO I AM

When I stopped needing other people to approve of me, I discovered that most of them liked me even more.

CONFESSION #863 …

I DECIDE WHAT I WANT FOR MY LIFE

I no longer look at other people and say "you need to change so that I can be happy". I look at them and say, "I am so in tune with Who I Am, that in my eyes you are perfect!"

CONFESSION #864 ...

I BLESS MY HOME

May our new home be a place of health, happiness and harmony for all who enter, a place where we are renewed, replenished and revitalized in each other's company, a place of growing and a place for sharing, a place for music and a place for laughter, a place of soft nurturing and gentle stimulation, a place to freely express love for each other, and a place where each person is appreciated, cherished, embraced, encouraged, honored and accepted for who they really are.

CONFESSION #865 …

I GET TO CHOOSE

I eat the foods I really like, I think the thoughts that make me feel good, I choose the emotions I enjoy the most, I go to places that give me a thrill, I hang around the people who make me feel better, I write the words that uplift my soul, I live in a place that stimulates appreciation, I enter the relationship that opens my heart.

CONFESSION #866 ...

I CONNECT TO MY SOUL

When a woman wants a man to step up and claim her, she doesn't do it effectively with words or conversation. SHE INVITES HIM with the softness of her energy, she calls him by releasing the tension in her heart, she lures him with the lightness of her walk and the brightness of her smile, she attracts him with the acceptance of all aspects of his natural masculine core, by acknowledging the strength, solidity and protection that he offers.

Enhanced by regularly nurturing of her own body, through the playfulness of her inner child, in the allowing of ALL her emotions, with the surrendering of control, in appreciation for life and laughter and love as she opens her deepest feminine divinity to receive him.

When she's ready and only then, she chooses consciously to connect to the "oneness" in her soul, washing away years of false bravado, revealing the nakedness of her yearning heart, and only those who can clearly hear her gentle whisper will answer the call.

And he will answer. HE WILL COME! He'll come when she is at her fullest. He'll answer with power, with passion, with a conviction she couldn't possibly deny.

Are you open to receiving the gifts he has to offer?

Welcome him with all your heart, for he too is uttering his own cry that only a woman who is truly open can hear.

CONFESSION #867 ...

I HAVE SIMPLE INTENTIONS

I intend to do whatever feels inspired, whatever brings me the most joy, whatever feels like the greatest fun, and whatever opens my heart even wider. I have no grand plan to change the world, help other people, save the animals or even to inspire you. Those things seem to happen as a natural result of just being MORE of ME!

CONFESSION #868 …

I GET OVER THINGS REALLY QUICKLY

I briefly acknowledge the problem, but look endlessly towards the solution.

CONFESSION #869 …

I FOUND MY PURPOSE IN LIFE

I once believed that life was about learning lessons, and then those lessons were presented over and over again until the pain got so bad, I had to CHANGE!

Now I know that the purpose of my life is to have more fun, and then opportunities for fun get presented over and over again until I get bored with the fun and decide to change the game.

> *"I always get to be right.*
> *My purpose is about what*
> *I DECIDE it will be!"*

CONFESSION #870 …

REAL LOVE STARTS WITH ME

It starts with accepting myself, no matter how bad I might feel in the moment, no matter how ugly I think I might look, no matter how many times I've failed, no matter how terrible I might have behaved and no matter what anyone else might think.

*"I accept Who I Am
and where I am,
right now!"*

CONFESSION #871 ...

I CAN GET HAPPY IN SO MANY WAYS

My happiness depends almost entirely on one thing: Choice! What am I choosing to give my attention to now!

- I CAN "Get Happy" by thinking my way there,
- I CAN "Get Happy" by writing my way there,
- I CAN "Get Happy" by playing my way there,
- But it's even easier to "Get Happy" by FEELING my way there.

CONFESSION #872 …

I LOOK WHERE I'M GOING

I don't want to go back to the way things were before; I just want to keep moving forward, towards the future of my dreams … ☺

CONFESSION #873 …

IT'S ALL WORTH IT

I don't mind what you're doing or thinking, I'm the one who sets my emotional tone, I'm the one who decides what it all might mean, I'm the one who imagines the way I want my future to be, I'm the one who finds value from everything I see.

CONFESSION #874 …

I KNOW HOW I LIKE TO FEEL

I only need to focus on that feeling and the pathway to everything I could possibly want for my future becomes clear.

- Taking a particular action makes me feel this way.
- Being with a special person makes me feel this way.
- Eating a certain food makes me feel this way.
- Choosing to specific topic makes me feel this way.
- Breathing deeply makes me feel this way.
- Loving with all my heart does it too.

CONFESSION #875 ...

MY MOOD DETERMINES MY RESULTS

WHEN I'M HAPPY ... I talk, I create, I imagine, I visualize, I fantasize, I write, I dream, I expand, I magnify, I solidify the vibe. I barely need to sleep at all.

WHEN I'M TIRED OR FLAT ... shhhhhh. I never add energy to an "out of the vortex" moment. I stay as quiet as I can and just let it run its course. Sleep is highly beneficial.

CONFESSION #876 …

I ALWAYS FIND WHAT I'M LOOKING FOR

So instead of looking for reasons to feel bad, I'm always looking for things that make me feel fabulous, I'm always looking for things to rock my world, I'm always looking for things to surprise and thrill me, I'm always looking for things to appreciate greatly, I'm always looking for ways to make everything fun and I'm always looking for even more reasons to flow my Love.

CONFESSION #877 …

I HAVE A POWERFUL IMAGINATION

- My imagination has produced a real live King straight out of a fairytale (that's what magical wishes can be used for).
- My Imagination has made friends from enemies (that's what thinking about the positive aspects can be used for).
- My Imagination has restored peace in a family (that's what remembering the good times can be used for).
- My Imagination has seen people who are close to me, reach the highest heights (that's what holding a vision can be used for).
- My Imagination has allowed money to materialize out of thin air (that's what faith can provide).
- My Imagination has created the most amazing opportunities by only focusing forward (that's what dreams are made of).
- My Imagination has transformed a friendship from mundane to sublime (that's what choosing to have as much fun as possible does).

- My Imagination has powerfully manifested a relationship that gives me abundantly more height, breadth and depth than I ever dreamed possible (that's what giving your most secret fantasies to God has the ability to do, in fact, I don't believe there's any other way).

"Empowered, Aligned and Passionately Me."

CONFESSION #878 …

A WISE MAN ONCE TOLD ME

When I think I need to work on my relationship; it's usually my finances that need more attention! When I think I need to increase my finances; it's usually my relationship that needs to thrive. When I think I'm missing something in both areas, it's usually time to go out and get happy, get high or get laid … ☺

CONFESSION #879 …

I'M ENJOYING MY LIFE SO MUCH

I don't care if I publish another book, buy the next luxury property, drive the new convertible, and cuddle up with my man who adores me completely. I can take a deep breath and feel totally free, walk out onto the beach and know the success that IS me, reach into the stillness and connect with "The Divine", touch my body and feel sensually sublime. I don't need manifestations to make me feel whole. I already AM, in Mind, Body and Soul.

CONFESSION #880 …

I PRAY IN A DIFFERENT WAY

I regularly pray prayers of appreciation, for everything I've already been given, for being alive right here, right now and for all the good things I don't know about yet. I appreciate not having to get my heart started each morning, I appreciate that the earth keeps rotating, that the sun keeps shining, that the oxygen keeps regenerating, that the plants keep growing. I appreciate how nature so naturally adapts to whatever we put her through. I appreciate the internet, mobile phone and the mind-blowing technology that enables us to communicate freely with people right around the globe in any moment we choose.

CONFESSION #881 …

I LIVE IN FOREVER LAND

- forever having fun,
- forever finding stuff to laugh about,
- forever dreaming about beautiful things,
- forever expanding my mind,
- forever creating magic,
- forever making love,
- forever getting high,
- forever living happily ever after …

… and the probability of you living happily after with me is really good too, because I'm really really happy, I'm really really fun, I'm really really aligned, I'm really really excited, I'm really really open, I'm really really focused, I'm really really passionate, I'm really really turned on, I'm really really loved up, I'm really really hot … lol … and I'm really really really really looking forward to co-creating more fabulous things with you too.

living & loving

Happily

EVER AFTER

CONFESSION #882 ...

LOVE IS ALL IN MY IMAGINATION

WE DON'T REALLY "FALL" IN LOVE ... We imagine our way to love.

We DON'T JUST MYSTERIOUSLY FALL OUT OF LOVE EITHER ... we focus our way there by concentrating on things that are nothing like what each person really is at their core.

ONCE THERE IS LOVE ... it always is and never ceases to be. Love can be expanded, reconstructed, enhanced, improved, grown, imagined and created out of almost nothing, but it can never be ignored entirely.

A RELATIONSHIP THAT SEEMS LIKE IT'S FALLING APART ... is just an indication that love has been temporarily pushed aside. This relationship has more potential to transform into something SO much better, than a relationship that just happens easy. There's nothing wrong with easy, but at the basis of all love is expansion and the deepest joy, and both are only possible by experiencing their opposite. The most profound way to develop a truly intimate bond is by choosing to move through the contrast/challenges and get to the other side (together).

BUT IT "DOESN'T" TAKE TWO ... to enhance a relationship beyond where it currently stands. It just takes ME to be willing to focus my attention and heart-felt energy with purposeful direction towards what I know inside is not only my deepest desire but one of the most fulfilling missions known to man/woman.

CONFESSION #883 …

I ONLY NEED TO REMEMBER 3 THINGS

1. I know who I am.
2. I know who you really are.
3. I know what God can do.

CONFESSION #884 …

I MAKE LIFE FUN

This is Elizabeth.
Elizabeth is wise.
She doesn't find fault with the government or with politicians. She'd rather put energy towards building people up not dragging them down. If she really wanted to make a big change, she'd run for office.
Be wise like Elizabeth.
VOTE 1 for FUN … ☺
Because when you make it fun,
it's a success before it's even begun.

CONFESSION #885 …

I EXPECT THE BEST FROM YOU

I doesn't matter what you do or say, I keep expecting the best from you anyway, and pretty soon, without any effort at all, you show me how amazing you really are, you show me how adaptable you can be, you show me how wide you can open your mind and you show me how enormously you can grow your heart, because that's who you really want to be too.

CONFESSION #886 …

THINGS CHANGE SO QUICKLY

A bad mood, can only last as long as my attention span. It's natural to feel good.

CONFESSION #887 …

I AM MAGNIFICENT

When I'm being my magnificent self, I feel all gooey and loving inside. I find the right words to speak. I can easily focus on the best in everyone. I effortlessly find the blessing contained in each experience. I'm solid and certain and sure of Who I Am. Then what I might want for the future doesn't even really matter anymore, as I am totally in the moment and loving everything, just as it is.

CONFESSION #888 …

I'M INFLUENTIAL

My real power to influence others, does not come from pointing out their mistakes, does not come from making them see they need to change and does not come from getting others to agree with me that their behaviour is inappropriate. My real power to influence comes simply by believing in them more than they believe in themselves, by imagining them living the life of their dreams and by showing them that perhaps, just perhaps, there might be another way.

CONFESSION #889 …

I ENHANCE EVERY RELATIONSHIP

The best thing I do to enhance my relationship is to believe my mate really is the incredible guy I love being with, to pretend he has every good quality I could possibly want and to treat him as if he is the most wonderful man in the world, and he just keeps proving that I'm right … ☺

CONFESSION #890 …

UNTIL FURTHER NOTICE

I'm celebrating everything!

CONFESSION #891 …

I HAVE THE KEY

The key to a successful relationship isn't to find the problems and try to iron them out (that just makes them bigger). The key is to FOCUS on the strengths, the connections and the amazing love we share and make them so much more significant, than anything that could possibly tear us apart.

CONFESSION #892 ...

I FALL IN LOVE OVER AND OVER AGAIN

FALLING IN LOVE ... is when I'm open to seeing the miracle inside you, often when you can't even see it yourself.

FALLING OUT OF LOVE ... is when I choose to STOP seeing the miracle inside you, and close down my own potential to imagine the best, to find the best and to draw out the best in both of us.

"I choose to Love".

CONFESSION #893 ...

I'M SUPPORTIVE

LIFTING YOU UP ... is when I imagine the best, find the best, acknowledge the best and draw out even more magnificent qualities, inside both of us.

PUTTING YOU DOWN ... is when I temporarily forget who we both really are inside.

"I choose to be supportive".

CONFESSION #894 …

I GIVE PEOPLE SPACE

HELPING YOU GROW … is when I give you space to decide what's right for you, when I trust you're receiving your own guidance too, when I accept your uniqueness is what makes life sublime, and allow you to find your own way too, just as I found mine.

RESTRICTING YOU … is when I try to tell you what's right from my own perspective and forget that the most important life we can ever forge, is our own.

"I choose to allow you the space to grow".

CONFESSION #895 …

YOUR STRENGTH BRINGS OUT THE BEST IN ME

I once thought I'd feel better when someone else loved me, but I really feel better when I'm around other people who "Love Themselves".

> "They showed me how to truly love, starting from the inside out."

CONFESSION #896 …

I ONCE THOUGHT THAT HONESTY WAS THE BEST POLICY

I've now found that if I don't have something uplifting to say about myself or another, it's better to say nothing at all.

> *"Unless asked for feedback, silence is a much better teacher than criticism will ever be."*

CONFESSION #897 …

I MADE MORE MONEY

The best thing I did that made me more money was when I stopped looking in my bank account for the results I "thought" I was seeking, and started noticing my heart expanding, because of the fun things I was doing, the joyful way I was giving and the delicious emotions I was feeling.

CONFESSION #898 …

I SEE MIRACLES EVERYWHERE

I don't need a miracle, to come before I wake up and notice how incredible life is. I just notice the miracles that are around me every day.

- The sun keeps coming up, that's a miracle.
- New lives are born, that's a miracle.
- My heart keeps beating, that's a miracle and now I was just inspired me to write another CONFESSION ... that's a miracle too ... ☺

CONFESSION #899 …

I DON'T NEED TO PROVE I'M WORTHY

I was worthy the moment I was born …

- worthy enough to enjoy the warmth of the sun,
- breathe the freshness of the air,
- feel the cleansing properties of the wind,
- see the magnificence of a rainbow,
- touch the softness of a babies skin,
- hear the sound of children laughing,
- smell the sweetness of the rain
- and know the goodness of life itself.

"ENTITLEMENT is born from a belief that you need to work hard to prove you "deserve" good things. WORTHINESS is realizing that goodwill naturally abounds, if you just let it in."

CONFESSION #900 …

I'M SATISFIED

Satisfaction is a feeling I can talk myself into, as I notice the beautiful things outside the window, the peace that exists in our home, the joy of spending time with animals and the good that's so abundantly obvious in our world.

CONFESSION #901 …

I LOVE KNOWING WHO I AM

When YOU really matter to yourself, when you know inside the value you have to give, when you are SO sure, SO knowing, SO certain of your own magnificence, whether someone in particular makes times for you or not, becomes completely irrelevant!

The right people for you are always just around the corner and you'll bump into each other in the very moment you let your expectation go of WHO it should be and allow Law of Attraction to bring you what you've REALLY been wishing for all along

CONFESSION #902 ...

I CREATE AFFINITY

NATURAL AFFINITY is when two or more people are on a similar wavelength and allow themselves to rise and fall with each other's moods/circumstances/experiences. The connection can be sustainable if desired, but the effects are unpredictable.

CONTRIVED AFFINITY is when someone imitates, assumes or imagines the body posture, movements and attitudes of someone else to gain a clearer understanding of where they're at;

- With intent to influence their mood. (Usually done in therapeutic situations, the connection is unsustainable, the effects are often detrimental to the therapist and any change is still totally in the hands of the client).

- With intent to get them to part with money, votes or something else considered to be of value. (Often done in sales, politics, cults and conditional relationships.)

Effects are determined by the person with strongest intent or agenda but can change in the instant the other decides what they really want for themselves.

- With intent to gain skills or insight into the success they've achieved. A strategy often called "Modeling" that tends to get sustainable results while the strategy is being implemented but needs to be integrated with the individual's most dominant vibration to be of any long term use.

VIBRATIONAL AFFINITY WITH ANOTHER is a natural attunement with the vibration of someone else. Each person we attract into our experience is emitting a similar vibration to us, whether we are consciously aware of it or not.

VIBRATIONAL AFFINITY WITH SOURCE is feeling your way through life and choosing thoughts, conversations and actions that personally feel better to you. The connection is always available and is best experienced when we're relaxed, calm and at peace. The effects rely on no other person to be different, no other condition to change and no other circumstance to be transformed for it to be felt. It is NOT meant to be sustained, just something which is either allowed or disallowed in any moment.

CONFESSION #903 ...

I MAKE THINGS BIGGER OR SMALLER

I don't have to change my circumstances. I just decide how significant I want them to be in the whole scheme of my life.

CONFESSION #904 …

I TRUST THE LAW OF ATTRACTION

Law Of Attraction always brings me a perfect match to what I'm REALLY thinking about, every time. Whether I've manifested illness or wellness, poverty or abundance, a loser or a lover, a rough patch or a smooth ride, it lets me know what I've been ignoring, what I've been oblivious to, what to change, what to focus upon and what to do.

"I appreciate this guidance more than anything."

CONFESSION #905 …

I AM THE QUEEN

I am Loving, I am Beautiful, I am Joyful, I am Kind, I am Expansive, I am Radiant, I have Peace and Clarity of Mind. I am Magnetic, I am Creative, I am Receptive, I am Inspiring, I am Original, I am Abundant, I am Graceful, I am Amazing.

I am Magnificent, I am Protected, I am Served and I'm Adored, I am Treasured, I am Admired and I am Supported even more. I am Grateful, I am Magical, I am Power, I am Light, I am Appreciative, I am Valuable, I am Wisdom, I have Insight.

I am Passion and Inspiration and Content I love to BE. I am in the Flow, I am Wealthy, I am Wise, I am ME! I am Present, I am Fulfilled, I am Perfectly Complete, My Emotions are Empowering, from the Heart I like to Speak. My Body, Mind and Spirit are in Total Harmony. I am Blissful, I am Ecstatic, I am Whole, I am FREE.

CONFESSION #906 …

I FOCUS ON WHAT I LOVE

If I don't like something about my life, I don't work out how I'm gonna fix it, I focus on what I LOVE about my life and let the solutions to those problems, come to me.

CONFESSION #910 …

I CHERISH HOW DIFFERENT WE ARE

Life would be boring if we all had the same values, chose the same lifestyle, adopted the same beliefs or adhered to the same rules, for without these differences I'd have no reason to grow my heart, no purpose to expand my ideas, no need to reach for a better way to LIVE IN HARMONY, and in total acceptance of your choices, whether I approve of them, understand them or would want to live that way or not.

CONFESSION #911 ...

I REMEMBER WHEN MY LIFE REALLY TOOK OFF

But I didn't get a new job, win the lottery, write another book, change my location or change my mate. I just kept on thinking about, talking about and getting involved in things that felt "right" to me ... without any judgment at all about what they were.

CONFESSION #912 …

I REMEMBER WHEN I FOUND MY TRUE PASSION

When I started doing something wholeheartedly, without needing any reward, without needing any acknowledgement, without needing to be paid, without needing anything in return other than the utter pleasure I got from being immersed in it … and discovered a passion that has great power, energy, prosperity and momentum contained in it.

CONFESSION #913 …

I REMEMBER WHEN I LEARNED TO TRUST

To trust my inner guidance completely.

When I'd had enough of starting things and never finishing them, when I'd had enough of feeling like crap when I woke up in the mornings, when I stayed in bed for weeks on end in deep depression, when I'd felt like my life wasn't even worth living. I knew there had to be something so much better than that, and I found it!

I made a new commitment to ME, to trust my inner guidance completely, and it's the most important commitment, that I've ever made.

CONFESSION #914 …

I REMEMBER WHEN I DECIDED TO "FOLLOW MY BLISS"

Without any judgment about what it might be, without worrying if anyone else would even approve, without doubt of how I would survive, without questioning if it had the potential to make me money and with total faith that "if it feels good, it must be good for me" … for the alternative was nothing short of hell on earth.

- If it feels good - it's guidance.
- If it feels bad - it's also guidance. Period!

CONFESSION #915 ...

I'M WISE

This is Elizabeth.

Elizabeth is wise.

She's an endangered species.

Save her! ... ☺

CONFESSION #916 …

I LIVE IN MY OWN LITTLE WORLD

THE WORLD I LIVE IN … doesn't doubt
what's possible,
or fear thinking something new.
I don't bother to follow the in-crowd
or even care about what's true for you.

I found out a long time ago
it's best to do what's right for me,
and focused on forging my path,
living in sync with my own integrity.

THE WORLD I LIVE IN … allows all others
to live in their own unique way,
I don't find need to disagree with anything
that you might think, do or say.

I just have a deep understanding,
of the way life works best for me,
and stand firm in the absolute knowing
that "I Create My Own Reality!"

CONFESSION #917 …

I ADMIRE AUTHENTICITY

While most people think that being "kind", "good" or "loving" is the best way to respond, I'd rather choose to be authentically me in each moment.

- If my city is being bombed, feeling vengeful might be an appropriate emotion, until it all passes naturally.
- If someone just stepped really hard on my foot, getting upset might be an appropriate emotion, until it all passes naturally.
- If I just got laid off from my job, blaming the government might be an appropriate emotion, until it all passes naturally.
- If my mate just died and left me with great debts, getting mad might be an appropriate emotion, until it all passes naturally.

Pre-deciding a response to always be loving is what often keeps women in abusive relationships.

Pre-deciding a response to always be kind is what keeps many kids getting bullied.

Pre-deciding a response to always be good is what stops a lot of people from enjoying really great sex.

Pre-deciding a response to not express their true feelings, is what keeps people down in depression.

"Have that if you want, but I'd rather be real".

CONFESSION #918 …

I CARE ABOUT WHAT WORKS

There are lots of things in the world that are uncomfortably true. But your power is contained always in what you choose to give your attention to. Cancer, war and really bad coffee is true, but continually complaining about them, getting other people to agree about the tragedy of it all and feeling sad does not serve anyone, least of all you.

You can't FIGHT against an existing reality and find PEACE. You can only find peace inside first then let uncomfortable thoughts of that past reality cease. I care not what other people think, do or say, and trying to encourage someone else to agree with me, is exactly what creates conflict, by expecting them to do things my way.

Change doesn't happen when lots of people agree, that just creates a minority. Change only occurs in the moment we allow, other people to choose what's right for them, in each moment, now.

"Groups who form out of a feeling of powerlessness, blame and anger do create momentum. But momentum that feels bad is like a ball rolling UP a hill. Momentum that feels good is unstoppable."

CONFESSION #919 …

I'M PROSPEROUS

I remember when I was training myself to have a more prosperous consciousness. When bills came in and I didn't know how I was going to pay them …

- The tendency was to look for ways to get bigger discounts,
- The tendency was to get involved in stupid conversations about the rising cost of living,
- The tendency was to react with a sense of dread and cut off my potential creativity,
- The tendency was to criticize what OTHER people/governments/corporations were doing with their money.

Then I developed a new tendency …

- I decided that when bills came in, instead of DOUBTING I could pay them, I just WONDERED what might happen
- I decided to give up the need to get discounts, to look for bargains, to shop in cheap stores

- I decided to remember how resourceful I can be,
- I decided to be more trusting of the power of God/Universe to draw more good things to me,
- I decided to do things that I loved, that felt good, that made me happy,
- I decided to stop listening to "the crowd",
- I decided to allow ideas, opportunities and creativity to flow.

Then I watched my world shift to match my new decisions …

- I spent so much less money because I was filling myself up with happiness, not with objects,
- People started giving me money for no reason other than it felt good,
- Incredible, ridiculously priced bargains for things I'd often dreamed of, showed up seemingly out of the blue,
- I wasn't charged for electricity for 12 months because of a mistake the power company made,
- Clients even to this day, put money in my account without me even billing them,
- Orders for future projects come in the mail,

- I was inspired to write like never before, in the middle of the night, in the middle of a date (that was funny), in the middle of conversations, words flowed with a clarity that often surprised even me.
- When I see something I want, I just let myself just want it PERIOD, and the ways and means are always provided.

Having a rich life wasn't something that happened because I worked hard (though when I'm inspired I can work joyfully for 24 hours straight and still want to do more), it didn't happen because I got lucky (though I feel phenomenally blessed), it didn't happen because I made the right investments (though the most incredible opportunities just keep finding me) and it didn't happen because I followed some master finance plan (my plan is to have fun, to be happy and to trust I'll be guided).

Prosperity is an inner journey first. When I gently trained my mind to recall more abundance stories, when I started choosing to get involved in conversations about how wonderful life can be and when I stopped comparing myself to others, life slowly started to feel better, and everything else is history.

CONFESSION #920 …

I LOVE GETTING BILLS

It means I have the ability to pay them.

I LOVE PAYING MY BILLS TOO

It means that prosperity is flowing in and out, in and out, in and out, like the air that I breathe.

CONFESSION #921 …

I'M SUCCESSFUL

My measure of success has nothing to do with how many people like my stuff, how many thousands of books I sell, how many clients keep asking for more, how many dollars I have in my bank account.

> *"My success is known intrinsically, in how "connected" I feel in each moment … ☺"*

CONFESSION #922 …

GOOD THINGS ARE GIVEN TO ME

I've never paid a cent for the sun to shine! I've never had to prove my worthiness so my heart would keep beating! I've never needed to add value to the forest or the beach or the birds or the trees and they don't expect anything in return either. I've never even had a thought that it was necessary to promote myself so I could be rewarded in some earthly way. I know profoundly my worthiness, and just ALLOW all the good stuff to keep flowing in ridiculous proportions.

"It's never been about how good I am. It's always been about how much I can allow."

CONFESSION #923 …

IT'S ALL GOOD

When I imagine that I can feel it, taste it, touch it smell it, see it, sense it and it feels really good to me, I don't need to make anything else happen, it's already done! Then there's nothing else to do but enjoy the sensations and allow the Universe to match the circumstances with how I already feel.

CONFESSION #924 …

I DON'T DO WHAT I SHOULD

I do what feels good! When I made that choice, life transformed from one of morbid obligation, to one of heavenly joy.

OBLIGATION ... is doing what "I assume" pleases others.

FREEDOM ... is doing what "I know" pleases me first, so I have infinitely more to give to others.

CONFESSION #925 …

I LAUGH AT MY PROBLEMS

Years ago we were taught that we should work on our issues, that we should delve right into them, that we had to get to the bottom of it all before we could really let something go.

Ha ha ha ha ha aha ha ha ha … oh wow, that was hard work.

But underneath, I always knew life was meant to be easier than that! So these days I quietly acknowledge the issue then just give it all to God/The Universe to handle for me. When I'm in that divinely trusting state I can relax again, I can laugh at it all, and the solutions just come, it all happens easily, and most often when I'm focused on something completely different.

CONFESSION #926 ...

I TAKE SHORT CUTS

I love having an easy life, so I don't bother to work at changing my negative thoughts and past beliefs anymore. Instead, I affirm "Who I Am" and where I'm going.

- I'm on the right track.
- I'm working things out.
- I'm doing pretty well.
- I'm feeling better and better.
- I'm growing, I'm expanding, I'm opening.
- I'm relaxing a lot more.
- I'm having a fun time here.
- I'm finding my sweet spot ... ☺
- I'm really good at what I do.
- I'm noticing welcome changes.
- I'm aware of the things that make my heart sing.
- I'm receiving guidance all the time.
- I'm doing what feels right for me.
- I'm being a leader, a lover, a light in the dark.
- I'm creating amazing things.
- I'm feeling incredibly free.

- I'm loving my self, my mind, my body, my life.
- I'm living in gentle alignment with my soul, in perfect tune with my own integrity.
- I'm happy, I'm healthy, I'm whole and complete.
- I'm glad I'm choosing to just be me!

CONFESSION #926 …

I'VE GROWN UP

I remember when I liked creating drama. When I'd deliberately push myself out of my comfort zone, when I'd provoke a conversation to get a reaction and when I'd experience all the highs and lows of a rollercoaster. It was fun.

Now I prefer a smoother, easier, more pleasurable ride. So I appreciate where I am, I just expect goods things to come, I've got a really solid foundation, I'm excited about what might happen, I know I can handle anything, I let the Universe bring me the thrills. I keep lifting myself even higher and find it sustainably exhilarating.

CONFESSION #927 …

I DON'T CARE ABOUT YOU

It's YOUR job to care about you!

In the moment I step in to care more for you than what you do for yourself, I take away YOUR power and give away my own. The best I can do is live as an example of what I believe, and by the clarity of my example, by shining the light, by illuminating the path, I set both of us free to be who we came to be … powerful, loving, intentional creators.

CARING IS TAUGHT BEHAVIOR

It usually started when our parents decided we should care more about what they wanted than for what we knew was right for us at the time. We were encouraged to move further away from our center, our Source, our Knowing, our Nature, simply because they had felt disconnected from their own ... Then we spend the rest of our lives trying to recover it!

When we do recover our natural nature, we end up being more authentic, more charismatic, more magnetic, more admired, more trusted, more thoughtful and the greatest role model of all ... one who lives in complete integrity with their own truth.

CONFESSION #928 …

I SEE THINGS DIFFERENTLY

While most people want to be with someone who loves "them" I like to be with a person who loves themselves.

While most people think that power is the ability to influence or control others, to me, real power is when I recognize instinctively that no situation is bad enough, no government is strong enough and no other person is manipulative enough to take away, change or misrepresent who I really am inside.

While most people work on overcoming their problems, I do my best to relax, remain calm, stay quiet, find peace and allow the solutions to be inspired "through" me.

While most people assume that it's best to face their fears, I use fear as my intuitive guidance and choose to turn towards what I love instead.

While most people are obsessed with talking about the realities of life, I'd rather focus on where I'm going, think about things that light up my life and share things that uplift all of us instead.

While most people believe that blame, anger and revenge are bad things, for anyone who's ever been grieving, in total despair, felt depressed or incredibly powerless, their life-giving properties are priceless. The emotions themselves are harmless and perfectly natural, but denying ourselves the 'right to express our feelings' is what really makes us go to extremes.

While most people set material, financial or success orientated goals, I set emotional goals! I know that having more stuff, or reaching a business milestone, or receiving an award makes me feel good temporarily, but the only reason I set those goals is because I think they'll make me feel good in the end, and if I do whatever it takes to feel good NOW, my goal is already achieved, instantly!

While most people believe death is a tragedy, I know it's always a blessing, a relief from trauma or a bodily condition, the release of emotional or mental pain, an opportunity to take life to another level. But continued suffering without relief, now that would be a tragedy.

What most people might consider to be a pity, a problem or a loss, I consider an opportunity in disguise, a change for the best, a chance to take a new adventure, a decision to get excited about what's unfolding magnificently before me. A time to take a leap of faith into knowing that EVERYTHING I've ever asked for is on its way to me right now, and in an even more incredible form that I could ever have imagined!

While most people believe that education provides the greatest opportunities for the future, I've found that I can't beat my imagination for being the primary catalyst, in taking me wherever I want to go.

While most people expect others to behave in certain ways, I just want you to be YOU, no matter where you're at, no matter what it might look like, no matter how negative it might be, because I KNOW you'll feel your naturally loving, kind and respectful self really soon, without me demanding that you get there right now! The more I allow you to just BE you, the more I allow me to just BE me too – authentic and real.

I want you to be "You" in your authentic and real state, not some contrived person like our parents, our teachers, our culture or our religion taught us to be. Just be who you really are, express where you're really at, and I know that pretty soon, you'll be feeling your magnificent self, all over again.

Most people start a relationship because they expect a mate will fulfill their needs, I choose to enter a relationship when most of my needs are already met and I have an abundance of "me" to give.

While most people try to avoid problems, I welcome them. Without hell, there would be no heaven. Without a problem, there would be no solutions. Without questions there would be no answers. Without eternal challenges, there would be no reason on earth to grow.

- If I'm feeling sad, I go out of my way to find happiness.

- If I can't pay my bills, I look for methods to create more money.

- If I'm feeling sick and tired, I come up with a solution to feel better and energized.

- If I want my freedom, I stop pretending I don't already have it.

While most people think they need money to survive, I rely on "Resourcefulness" more than anything else. I can entertain people and get attention. I can write a book and feel important. I can quieten my mind and experience bliss. I can be myself and feel free. I can use my imagination to travel anywhere I want. I can collect veges from the garden and cook up a feast … OR I can stop for a moment, feel my wholeness, acknowledge that *I Am Enough*, and let it deeply feed my soul.

While most people care about what others might think of them, I care only about what I think of me!

CONFESSION #929 …

I LINE UP WITH THE SOLUTION

This is Elizabeth.
Elizabeth is wise.
She knows that during the toughest times when things get rough,
she reminds herself what the purpose of life really is.
Be wise like Elizabeth.
Simply get on with it, find ANY way to be happy …

… and buy more damn shoes … ☺

CONFESSION #930 ...

I LOVE TO HAVE IT ALL

DO I WANT TO MAKE A COMMITMENT OR DO I WANT MY FREEDOM? ... I can have it all. I can make a commitment and still be completely free to focus my attention on things that make me feel alive, that make me feel good, that make me feel whole.

DO I WANT TO GO TO WORK OR DO I WANT TO GO TO THE BEACH? ... I can have it all. I can go to work with such a great attitude and energize myself so much, that I can physically do both and even more.

When I'm faced with a decision like this, I always choose both. I know that anything is possible when I find that trusting feeling, when I put my limitations aside, when I hand it over to the Universe and just let it come.

CONFESSION #931 …

I DON'T NEED TO MAKE THINGS HAPPEN

Life gets so much easier every time I STOP trying to "make" something happen and start focusing on what I WANT and why I want it. There's often a better road that takes me towards my desires and when I trust it will be shown to me, the way is always paved so well I stand back in awe.

CONFESSION #932 ...

I ASK THE RIGHT QUESTIONS

I don't ask, will I get what I want? I prefer to ask, how much fun will I have? How much pleasure will I feel? How thoroughly thrilling will it be?

I just expect wonderful things to happen and the questions I ask the Universe determine the quality of my experience. They define a much clearer focus and set the standard for everything that comes to me.

CONFESSION #933 …

I TAKE CONTROL

I care so much about this moment, that I won't waste a second of it worrying about something I can't possibly control, and that's everything except MY thoughts, MY focus, MY words and MY actions.

CONFESSION #934 ...

I KNEW I'D GOT THE DEEPER MESSAGE

- When it felt better to remain faithful, even if someone wasn't being faithful to me.

- When I stopped being negative, about other people who were often very negative.

- When I held back my criticism, of those who were prone to criticizing.

- When I allowed other people to be themselves, even if they didn't like it when I was being me.

- When I refused to gossip, about others who were often sharing bad news.

- When I gave up trying to understand, the individuals who just didn't seem to understand.

- When I stopped noticing what I thought was wrong with other people, and just stayed true to what feels "right" for me.

CONFESSION #935 …

YOU HAVE EVERYTHING YOU NEED RIGHT NOW

You don't need to buy another book, go to another seminar, get advice from an expert or try harder at anything at all.

If you want something >> hope for it >> activate it >> imagine the fun of it >> feel good about it >> enjoy it >> affirm it >> believe it >> trust it >> know it >> It's done!

But here's the trick, only think about it while it feels good or get off the subject completely and think about something that feels so much better instead.

Creation happens whenever strong emotion is activated, both pleasant and unpleasant. YOU are the expert of your life. If it feels good, just do it, if it doesn't, let it go.

CONFESSION #936 …

CONTRAST MAKES ME APPRECIATE THINGS SO MUCH MORE

I'm so glad I wasn't born into riches or I'd never appreciate fully everything I have right now, I'd never completely understand the process of how I got from there to here and I might never have had the intense pleasure of reaching for something incredibly alluring, and then moving positively towards it.

*"They were right all along:
The Joy really is in the Journey!"*

CONFESSION #937 ...

I KNEW I WAS IN THE MIDDLE OF REAL ABUNDANCE

1. When I let myself own a gorgeous car (instead of only buying financial investments) and praised myself and all the Universe, every time I see it, drive it or even think about it.

2. When I could throw out expensive clothes without feeling guilty (instead of handing them down), and then celebrate whole heartedly every time I value the beauty, quality and simplicity of what I have left.

POVERTY MENTALITY ... assumes some are born less fortunate than others.

ABUNDANCE MENTALITY ... knows we only have to ask, and it is given.

CONFESSION #938 …

I LOVE MONEY

- I DON'T SPEND MONEY … I circulate it.

- IT'S NEVER GONE FOR GOOD … it keeps coming back.

- I LOVE TO LET IT GO … and declare, "There's plenty more where that came from!"

- I BREATHE LIFE, LOVE AND MONEY … in and out, in and out.

- I HAVE SO MUCH FUN WITH MONEY … it just can't resist my company.

CONFESSION #939 …

I HAVE A LIFE OF TOTAL & UTTER FREEDOM

REAL FREEDOM is when I can make a commitment to a relationship and remember I'm free to focus on whatever aspects of the other person I choose, no matter how they're behaving.

REAL FREEDOM is when I can feel obligation to do work that may have lost its inner appeal but still know I'm free to focus on acknowledging the incredible outer benefits as well.

REAL FREEDOM is when I can be in a country where lots of things might appear as if they're unjust, unconscionable and unfair but deliberately take the time to feel the freedom of imagining how they could be instead.

REAL FREEDOM is when I can live in a world where there's tragedy, trauma and strife and realize I'm still free to enjoy the ever-present beauty of nature, the joyful laughter of children, the scent of a flower, the abundance of fresh air, the warmth of a smile, the conversations that uplift everyone and let myself settle into a feeling of appreciation for the dominant goodness that always abounds.

REAL FREEDOM is when I remember that I am responsible for whether I'll keep focusing on the problems or give my attention to solutions, whether I'll get bogged down by concentrating on someone's weaknesses or lift everybody up by expanding on our strengths, whether I'll do things out of obligation or feel the freedom to do them because I've had fun finding ways to live life with joy, with appreciation, with eagerness, with positive expectation, with the love that I am – no matter what!

CONFESSION #940 ...

A GOOD MAN ADDS SO MUCH TO MY LIFE

Especially, to help settle my emotions.

Men also have a lot to teach women if we shut up for a while and allow them to express themselves fully, without needing to tell our side of the story, without judging their method of delivery, (the more passionate or angry they get the more they actually care) and without walking out on them.

There is a distinction to be made here though. A GOOD MAN whose opinion is valuable is a respectful man, one who treats all the women in his life well, who's willing to face the wrath of our reaction because he feels strongly enough to tell us when certain behavior is inappropriate.

Often these men are labeled by younger, more inexperienced women as controlling or even narcissistic. That's ok, just be aware that both men and women tend to label or objectify things they don't understand until they're ready to shift their perspective and find the positive intent at the basis of every persons actions - no exceptions!

These good men are everywhere. They are usually older, with distinguished characters and a strong sense of self. They possess a deep wisdom that I have recently come to be openly in awe of and realize how much I need them in my life, because their presence on this planet adds a quality, balance and completeness that is not available anywhere else.

When we stop treating each other as the enemy and appreciate the perfection of our God-Given differences, we'll know the POWER of true partnership.

CONFESSION #941 ...

I DON'T HATE ANYONE

Not the terrorists, not Hitler, not suicide bombers, not pedophiles, not the government and certainly not someone I once loved dearly.

Hate ISN'T a natural emotion! It's a response that anyone can choose in any moment for any reason. It's just not a response I would personally choose ever.

Hate eats away at your physical body, is one of the underlying vibrational causes of cancer, heart attacks and accidents. When something upsetting has happened I don't pretend I can love in that moment. I just choose confusion instead and trust that clarity and understanding will find me soon enough.

CONFESSION #942 …

I'M NOT DRIVEN BY SUCCESS

I'm inspired by HaPpYnEsS.

CONFESSION #943 ...

I CAN SMILE IN AN INSTANT

If unpleasant stuff has my attention, just contemplating the potential benefits, is enough to bring me Peace, and a Smile ... ☺

CONFESSION #944 ...

I CELEBRATE OFTEN

I'M REDUCING THE NEED TO BRAG ... and replacing it with "a desire to celebrate!"

BRAGGING IS ... trying to prove you're better than someone else which anchors a mixed feeling of superiority/inferiority.

CELEBRATING IS ... achieving an improvement for yourself and anchoring a great feeling of success.

People in our culture once taught it was bad to brag and stopped celebrating altogether. But celebrating small wins, most definitely, invites the appearance of BIG successes.

CONFESSION #945 ...

IT'S NOT MY JOB TO LOVE YOU

It's my task to love myself so much that when you look into my eyes, you'll see your own magnificence shining back at you.

CONFESSION #946 ...

DOING LESS GETS ME MORE

- More allowing, less demanding.
- More relaxing, less trying.
- More playing, less working.
- More fun, less struggle.
- More trusting, less questioning.
- More flowing, less efforting.
- More inspiration, less need for motivation.
- More humor, less seriousness.
- More sex, less frustration.
- More being, less doing.
- More awareness, less obliviousness.
- More inspiration, less need for motivation.
- More openness, less need for closure.
- More living, loving and laughing than ever before.

CONFESSION #947 ...

WHEN I NEED TO SLOW DOWN

It doesn't take much for the momentum to swing the other way; a deeper breath, a lighter thought, a gentler approach, a hearty laugh, a calmed mind, a soothing word, a silly smile, a ridiculous joke, a different angle, a relaxed body, a broader perspective, a quieter response, a heartfelt apology, a moment of connection, a simple tear.

"Gentle change starts here!"

CONFESSION #948 ...

I FALL IN LOVE EVERY DAY

Being in love is a choice I make every day, by not letting silly issues get in the way. Taking more notice of what I'm currently giving attention to, taking time to acknowledge the special moments shared between me and you.

Expanding the fun stuff and letting go the rest, never ever putting your motives to the test. I now trust our deeper intentions are always aligned, and it's liberating to stop expecting either of us, to be so perfect at any time.

CONFESSION #949 ...

MY LIFE IS EXPANDING AND I'M GOING WITH IT. YAY.

- I've decided to enjoy the contrast!

- I love my emotions.

- I love it when things don't go exactly how I thought they might.

- I love how the Universe surprises me with something way way better every time.

- I love it that I've had enough experience to know this is preparing me for the magic that's still to come.

- I love that I can shift my feelings from one state to another simply by writing things that make proper sense.

- I love my guidance telling me when something I'm thinking is "off"

- I love focusing on what I want instead.

- I love the incredible power this process gives me.

- I love having received the vision for my/our path.

- I love knowing that Source has got this handled.

- I love knowing that my real job is to relax and enjoy the ride.

- lol ... did someone mention contrast?

- Man, this is really, really fun!

- Best energy movement EVER!

- Stepping back onto the Magic. Right where I belong

CONFESSION #950 ...

I'VE IDENTIFIED THREE TYPES OF LOVE

FEAR BASED LOVE ... needs commitment, rules and guidelines in order to feel safe to share its energy, and only does so with those who can be manipulated to comply with the required conditions.

MUTUAL LOVE ... needs regular attention and nurturing or else it will seek someone new to share its energy with.

DIVINE LOVE ... requires nothing from anyone else at all. It IS the light, it is the source, it is enough.

CONFESSION #951 ...

I CAN CHANGE WHAT I'M ATTRACTING

I CAN CHANGE WHAT I'M ATTRACTING ... In the moment I stop thinking about the things I haven't got and start remembering what I have.

I CAN CHANGE WHAT I'M ATTRACTING ... when I stop concentrating on the problem, take a deeper breath, quieten my thoughts and relax into the solution.

I CAN CHANGE WHAT I'M ATTRACTING ... when I stop being so hard on myself.

I CAN CHANGE WHAT I'M ATTRACTING ... when I let myself be, right where I am without trying to change anything at all.

I CAN CHANGE WHAT I'M ATTRACTING ... by not aiming for anything in particular, other than a feeling of RELIEF. Ahhhhhh, that feels a little better already.

I CAN CHANGE WHAT I'M ATTRACTING ... by reminding myself that nothing lasts forever, by remembering how things have always worked out before and by telling myself, "it'll all be over soon!"

I CAN CHANGE WHAT I'M ATTRACTING … when I stop TRYING so hard to be perfect, loving, kind, grateful, compassionate or understanding and just be real!

I CAN CHANGE WHAT I'M ATTRACTING … when I stop asking the question and be open to receiving the answer. What I've asked for has already been given.

I CAN CHANGE WHAT I'M ATTRACTING … When I stop giving someone else the credit for my happiness OR the blame for my unhappiness. One is no better than the other … I'm responsible for both.

CONFESSION #952 ...

I'M ALL FOR EQUAL OPPORTUNITY

But equal opportunity isn't achieved when I align with others to boost the energy of a minority; that leads to even further feelings of powerlessness.

Equal opportunity is when I align with my own Inner Knowing and recognize instinctively that no situation is bad enough, no government is strong enough and no other person is manipulative enough to take away, change or misrepresent who I really am inside, remembering that EVERY other person has that same opportunity too, to come into alignment with the greatest power of all … their own!

CONFESSION #953 …

THIS IS HOW VIBRATION WORKS IN OUR LIVES

- Spirit/Source/God energy current flows at the basis of the entire Universe.
- That Energy IS US.
- When you regularly invite that power into your life, there is not one debilitating illness that you cannot come back from.
- There is not one serious relationship breakdown that you cannot find harmony in.
- There is not one major bout of depression that you cannot rise from.
- There is not one situation at any time in life that cannot be enhanced and not only enhanced, but brought to a place of expanding the Universe in a phenomenally profound way with enormous personal, cosmic and spiritual growth.

Do whatever it takes to FEEL that connection. Your life will never be the same!

Welcome Source in again Today
YOU DESERVE IT!

CONFESSION #954 ...

I CELEBRATE THE SMALLEST OF WINS

MOST PEOPLE WANT SUCCESS *NOW* ... but the fact is, if you can't acknowledge the small successes you're having already, you aren't prepared spiritually to receive more.

HOW TO BE SUCCESSFUL ... There's a big difference between someone who's "trying" to make it big and someone who's practicing "being" a success. One is pushing energy out, the other is attracting energy back. There are so many universal forces working for us every step of the way. Just do what you love to do and let success find you. ~ ER

MAKE THE MOST OF THE TALENTS YOU HAVE ... There's a big different between working on your weaknesses and capitalizing on your strengths. One keeps energy firmly focused on the existing problem the other propels you freely towards the future.

Concentrate on doing the things you love and watch how all the universal forces, assist you from above.

CONFESSION #955 ...

I LOVE DIETS

This is Elizabeth.
Elizabeth is on a special LOVE diet.
She's been told to love who she is.
She's been told to appreciate what she's got.
She's been told that everything she needs is inside her right now.
Well ... now that fabulous muffin she just spotted in the bakery window is inside her too ... 😀

CONFESSION #956 ...

I DO WHAT I WANT TO DO

Once I start something new it never matters that I don't have all the steps planned out, in fact, I think it's better that way. I'm getting such strong guidance every moment of the day. If it's thrilling, if it rocks my world, if it sets my soul on fire, then that's the clearest guidance I could possible desire.

I never cared for what was popular, what others might advise, following a gurus plan or doing what my parents thought was wise, I always did what I wanted to do, what lit my fire, what sang to my soul, what got my juices flowing and what made me feel whole.

CONFESSION #957 ...

I FOLLOW MY OWN PATH

- TO MAKE MONEY ... I follow a plan.

- TO BE HAPPY ... I follow my bliss

- TO PROVE MYSELF RIGHT ... I follow my beliefs.

- TO BE A CREATOR ... I follow my dreams.

CONFESSION #958 ...

I MAKE MY RELATIONSHIP WORK FOR ME

It's easy to search for the best possible mate and expect to have the best possible relationship. But it's so much more fulfilling to allow my current relationship to transform into the most important, most dynamic, most loving and most expansive co-creative experience that takes place in my entire lifetime.

CONFESSION #959 ...

I ENJOY THE PROCESS

- I make a decision - I want it!

- I'm willing to let momentum build - I'm lining up with it!

- I'm trusting the way will be shown - I have faith in it!

- I'm allowing it to come - I'm guided towards it.

- I'm so excited - I'm feeling the intense pleasure of it!

- When action is inspired - I just can't stop it!

- The joy is in the journey - I'm so so so so so glad I waited for it!

CONFESSION #960 ...

MY LIFE IS OUT OF CONTROL

So I've handed the finer details over to a Higher Power to manage for me. And I know without a shadow of a doubt that no matter what my bank account says, no matter what state the economy is in, no matter what drama is going on in the world, no matter how my mate is behaving, my real job is to find as many things as possible to love and appreciate about what I HAVE right now.

CONFESSION #961 ...

LOVE FEELS GOOD

If it doesn't feel good you've turned it into something else. Expectation hurts, trying to be tolerant hurts, closing down your heart hurts, focusing on someone else's negative behavior hurts, beating up on yourself hurts, not being honest about how you're really feeling hurts and withholding love hurts you more than anything else.

Allow your emotions to just be, and watch them flow through you with great speed. Just like children out to play, spontaneously express what they're feeling, but don't let it get in the way.

Emotions are guidance, letting us know if we're looking forward or back. Don't condemn them or control them, just use them to keep you on track. If it feels good, your thoughts are aligned. If it feels "off", go relax with a walk, a good book, a glass of wine. Pretty soon you'll be feeling better again. Well-being is natural, just get back on the train.

CONFESSION #962 ...

IF I WANT SOMETHING I GIVE IT TO MYSELF FIRST!

If I want RESPECT, I make sure I'm treating myself well.

If I want MORE MONEY, I make sure I'm doing things that help me feel truly abundant.

If I want to be LOVED, I take time out to connect with the Source inside me that has an infinite supply of love to give and let the other people I've been holding responsible for how I'm feeling, off the hook completely.

CONFESSION #963...

I DON'T MEASURE SUCCESS BY YOUR LEVEL OF WEALTH

I measure success by your level of happiness with what you've been given, your appreciation for what you have now and your excited anticipation of what's still to come.

CONFESSION #964 ...

I DON'T CONSIDER BEING IN A RELATIONSHIP ANY MEASURE OF SUCCESS

But I do consider how happy you are with what you have as the greatest indication of its impending longevity.

CONFESSION #965 ...

TO FIND OUT IF I'M ON MY CHOSEN PATH

I think less and feel more.

Does this thought feel better? Does this action feel better? Does this conversation feel better? Does this story make me feel better or does it keep me stuck in the past?

My center is based in my heart. My balance comes from integrating heart and mind. My power comes from synergy between heart, mind and soul.

CONFESSION #966 ...

I VALUE THIS MOMENT

A PROFOUND MOMENT ... is having deep insight or understanding that I'm still catching up with.

BEING IN THE MOMENT ... is having deep insight or understanding that feels like the most natural process in the world.

CONFESSION #967 ...

I KNOW MY VALUE

This is Elizabeth.
Elizabeth is outraged!
...
...
Oh hang on.
That must be a misprint.
...
...
Elizabeth is outrageous, witty, enchanting, funny and never humble.

Be like Elizabeth.
KNOW YOUR WORTH,
so you never settle for less than what you and this magical Universe has the ability to provide… when you are truly open to receive!

CONFESSION #968 ...

I CHOOSE WHO I SPEND TIME WITH

It's gotta feel deliciously right or it will likely go annoyingly wrong.

CONFESSION #969 ...

I'M SELFISH

I consider my relationship with my own "Inner Contentment" to be the most important of all. When I am aligned, when I am in Love with life, when I am being who I want to be, I have the most value to give to my friends, to my enemies, to my loved ones and to the world.

CONFESSION #970 ...

FOCUSING IS THE MOST IMPORTANT WORK YOU'LL EVER DO

- If something feels pleasant, move towards it. THAT'S EASY.

- If something feels unpleasant, use that as a springboard to choose something that feels so much better. THAT'S YOUR WORK.

"That's what determines your level of happiness. That's what defines your path. That's what creates your reality."

CONFESSION #971 ...

SIX OF THE BEST TIPS YOU'LL EVER RECEIVE

1. Do what you love to do.

2. Do whatever it takes to feel good.

3. When something feels good, it's an indication you're on your path. If it doesn't feel good, it's indicating resistance in some form.

4. Don't work on the resistance (that just makes it bigger), concentrate on what does feel good and make that bigger instead.

5. Know that you and I and everyone else has a direct connection to "Source Energy". Use it. That's where the best ideas, the simplest solutions and the greatest advice comes from.

6. You don't need me. You have all the resources of the Universe at your fingertips. Have faith the path will continue to be shown to you. You are magnificent.

CONFESSION #972 ...

CONTRAST IS MY INDICATOR

Attracting contrast doesn't mean you're a bad person. Enjoying a happy moment doesn't mean you're good. It's just an "indication" of where your energy is currently at, that's all!

"Life is meant to be fun and contrast is just part of the variety."

CONFESSION #973 ...

I ENJOY THE FEELING WHEN SOMEONE DIES

I shift my energy straight into love and appreciation for their contribution to my life and enjoy a rip roaring conversation with their spirit. It's totally your choice whether you see death as a loss (and let your emotions spiral downwards) or, allow it to be a "Glorious Blessing" and connect in a stronger way than ever.

"We are eternal beings after all!"

CONFESSION #974 ...

WHEN I DIE, THROW A PARTY

I'll be celebrating along with you!

CONFESSION #975 ...

I ONCE CHARGED TO BE A THERAPIST

But there's a tendency to keep people stuck in the issue long enough so they feel obligated to pay our fee. These days I don't ask for a cent, now those who show up move to the solution so quickly, they often "gift" me ridiculous sums of money out of appreciation.

I've had people chase me for bank account details. A lady sent cash and a card in the post when I softly refused. So many others make spontaneous deposits. One guy turned up at my building just recently with a fistful of cash.

It's the most satisfying way to work … unconditionally … I love to have fun, so I only pick the ones that are aligned with the way I fly. Life was meant to be easy.

I also want to change the word "clients" to co-creators. I get as much value from our interactions as they probably do. I feel like I've been paid in fun before I've even begun.

CONFESSION #976 ...

I HAVE A BIG SECRET

Although I have everything I could possibly need, I do get a thrill out of being a "kept woman!"

CONFESSION #977 ...

I'M TOTALLY DEBT FREE

How did I get there? I have no idea. I only know what I didn't do.

- I certainly didn't work at it ... I play all day.

- I didn't envy people with lots of money ... but I get immense pleasure from being happy with what I have.

- I didn't set any big goals ... but I do spend hours dreaming.

- I didn't make a specific plan ... I just got in the habit of taking things easy.

- I didn't aim for wealth ... but I really, really, really appreciate luxury.

- I didn't hang out with rich people, in rich places, living rich lifestyles ... I find incredible richness in living simply. Truly.

- I didn't follow a gurus advice ... I thrive on listening to my own internal guidance.

- I didn't long for a better tomorrow ... I value where I am in every moment.

- I didn't worry about how I'd support myself when I got older ... I trusted things would work out one way or another.

- I didn't try to be better than anyone else ... I concentrated only on improving my mood.

- I didn't focus on manifesting material objects ... but I sometimes focus on how they might make me feel if I had them right now.

- But MOST OF ALL, I AIM to HAVE FUN ... and whenever I do that, even more good stuff comes.

P.S. It all sounds too easy. Maybe I should go back and formulate the steps and package it into an online program, run workshops, build an email list, pay for an autoresponder. Oh hang on! I already have everything I could possibly want, with more good stuff on the way! ... ☺

CONFESSION #978 ...

I DON'T SPEAK BADLY ABOUT OTHERS

Not because I'm trying to be a goody-goody, but because it stuffs up my own energy, every time I do.

CONFESSION #979 ...

I KNOW WHAT LOVE IS

LOVE ... doesn't bring you to your knees so someone can walk all over you. That's resignation!

LOVE IS STRENGTH ... Love says, I love us both so much that I won't let you try and manipulate me, I won't let you take advantage of me, I won't let you put me down, I won't let you be less than the amazing person I know you really are.

CONFESSION #980 ...

MY GOAL ACHIEVING PROCESS

1. I'm here. I want to be "Here".

2. Let the fun begin.

3. Works every time! .. ☺

CONFESSION #981 ...

I NEVER CONDEMN AN ADDICTION

That keeps it firmly in place.

Addiction is simply a momentum of energy which is far far far easier to change by changing your "vibe" than by any physical action you decide to take.

STEPS TO TAKE

1. Go easy on yourself.

2. Tell yourself, it's just "momentum of energy" which YOU can redirect in a short space of time (3 - 30 days).

3. Realize that feeling good, looking good and treating yourself good is what you've been wanting all along.

4. Ask yourself, "What is it that makes me feel truly empowered or loving or centered or strong?" (Usually a spiritual practice)

5. When you're ready, make a decision to do

10 -15 minutes of this practice each morning BEFORE you start your day for at least 30 days.

6. Remember to go easy on yourself. "Punishment has never been responsible for long term change, only love can do that!"

7. Watch what happens next ... you are magnificent.

CONFESSION #982 ...

I LOVE TO GET GOOD RESULTS

- I prefer to attract rather than promote.

- I prefer to inspire rather than control.

- I prefer to bring out your positive side than condemn your bad one.

- I prefer to lift people/corporations/governments up rather than put them down.

- I prefer to quietly remove myself from a stressful situation until I find peace, rather than loudly profess my rightness and add fuel to the heat.

*"That's the only demonstration
I'm interested in!"*

CONFESSION #983 ...

I DON'T BELIEVE IN MONOGAMY AS A RULE

I give it as a gift. It's a gift I give to myself, to keep directing my focus positively on one mate, for in doing this, I empower the greatest relationship of all ... full connection of my heart, my mind and my soul with the Source of life.

And if for some reason I slip into negativity, I don't go outside myself to find relief, I go peacefully inside until I regain my footing, and return, to the love I know exudes from my soul.

CONFESSION #984 …

I ENJOY MAKING UP WITH MY MATE

I overlook the need for an apology. Can I instead tempt you to smear freezing cold ice-cream over my body as punishment for whatever you think I've done wrong?

I dunno, maybe some gentle spanking might be in order too … ☺

Sexual healing has far more success than discussing issues can possibly overcome as it takes us out of our minds and connects us to a more spiritually fulfilling place, where the solution to everything, most naturally resides.

CONFESSION #985 ...

I BELIEVE IN DISCIPLINE

This is Elizabeth.

Elizabeth believes strongly in discipline.

But she's usually wearing tall black boots, and a slightly wicked grin ... while she's doing it ... ☺

CONFESSION #986 ...

I CHOOSE EMPOWERING MEANINGS

When something happens, it means, whatever you want it to mean. So make it mean something that feels freakin' good.

- You're on track.
- Something better is coming.
- This is preparing me for my next adventure.
- There's more good stuff where that came from.
- I'm getting wiser.
- That helps me get clearer.
- What a great opportunity to start again.
- Nothing ends, it just keeps evolving.
- Bring it on! I can handle anything.

Finding a way to FEEL good about what's happened makes the journey super delicious - right now.

CONFESSION #987 ...

IF I'M HAPPY WITH MY RESULTS

I change nothing!

CONFESSION #988 ...

I CAN ONLY RECEIVE WHAT I CAN ALLOW

MOST PEOPLE PRAY. .. for something specific that they aren't currently lined up to receive.

I ASK TO RECEIVE ... whatever I'm presently able to let in.

CONFESSION #989 ...

GOD IS PROVIDING FOR ME AT ALL TIMES

- Have I lined my energy up to receive it?

- Do I believe it's coming?

- Am I expecting it to arrive?

- Or am I still trying to prove I'm worthy?

"Now that's the question!"

CONFESSION #990 ...

I LIKE TO ...

Notice what's working. Look for what's right. Sense some sizzling sensations. Go after the things that shine bright.

Be with people who are happy. Trust others to find their own way. Give when I FEEL inspiration. Remain quiet when there's nothing to say.

I LIKE TO ...

Bask in ALL of life's pleasures. Open to guidance from above. Dance as if the music has no ending. Let my heart overflow with great love.

Live each moment with appreciation, anticipating better things to come. Realize I have more than I could possibly want, when all I do is, decide to "Have Fun!"

CONFESSION #991 ...

I CAN FOCUS ON ONE SMALL POSITIVE THOUGHT

And turn my whole day around.

CONFESSION #992 ...

I KNOW WHEN I'M READY

A feeling of calm confidence pervades my body. You can't fake it with words, (in fact words spoken too soon hold it away longer), but you can work up to it through e-motion.

> *"Fun. Laughter. Lightness. Joy. Stillness, Calm and Peace."*

CONFESSION #993 ...

I NEVER SUFFER

SUFFERING COMES ... from holding on too tightly to the way you think things should be.

FREEDOM COMES ... from letting go and allowing things to become, even better.

CONFESSION #994 ...

LIFE IS WHAT I MAKE IT

No one needs a life-coach, a therapist, a library of books, endless study material, a guru, a seminar or anything else to enjoy life to its fullest. I was NOT meant to struggle, to strive, to fight for my place, to work hard, to face fears, to do it tough. Life is meant to be fun, to feel good and be enjoyed.

CONFESSION #995 ...

I AM A *USER*

I USE MY MATE ... as an outlet to flow love, as a reason to open my heart and expand my mind. I use him for sex, the beautiful things he provides, company during the day, fabulous dinners at night, to appreciate his thoughtful gifts and help define what I desire to create in the future. I use him to provide for me in ways that encourage growth and contribution ... and that make him feel proud.

I USE FACEBOOK ... as a place to have fun, as a platform to meet others, as a way to share my thoughts, as a distraction from stress, as a method to practice my writing and as a source of brilliant entertainment.

I USE YOU ... to provide inspiration, to broaden my skills, to enhance my fulfilment, to draw answers through me, to give me the best reason to be here and explore my own purpose for living.

I USE GOD ... to guide me (through my emotions), to give me wisdom (through my mind), to live through me (through my physical body), to inspire me (through my soul) and to help me contribute profoundly to the expansion of the entire Universe.

CONFESSION #996 ...

I'M NOT NORMAL, IT'S TRUE

Sometimes I'm even downright weird.

So when someone tells me that the economy is poor, I say, lucky I'm not normal. I have a different way of looking at it! When someone tells me love should be about "give and take", I say, lucky I'm not normal. I have my own way of BEING it! When someone tells me they need me to behave in a certain way so they can feel secure/safe/loved, I say, lucky I'm not normal. I support you in finding it!

I love it. I care less and less what they think. I've make my weirdness not only work for me but jet-propel me into the future I CHOOSE to have.

CONFESSION #997 ...

THE BEST PART OF LIFE IS YET TO COME

When I'm enchanted by the future and not obsessed with the past, life takes on new meaning where no dark shadows can be cast. There's not one thing I can dream of that cannot be given, by this abundant Universe … vibrationally driven.

When I feel positive emotion all good things are drawn, towards me with haste, soon after the thought has been born. To live life with forward vision of what's possible to create, is more fulfilling than talking about the past for heaven's sake.

When the time comes to ask someone, "how have you been?" Instead I prefer to say, "Tell me your dreams!" It inspires a more unique conversation, I'd say and helps BOTH of us have a much brighter day.

You see, everything happens because of how we are feeling. You know that positive emotions all inspire healing. Let the next words you speak be of happiness and hope, and not about how you're worried you won't cope.

There's one important piece of advice I'd like to impart … to let the power of the Universe be called through your heart. Whatever you are wanting, relax your mind and allow, yourself to feel it as if you already have it right now.

No longer speak of the bad stuff … but let the good memories remain. When you live like this, things will never be the same. Our future hopes and dreams still keep calling us home, for the very best part of life, is yet to come.

CONFESSION #998 ...

I FILL MYSELF UP

This is Elizabeth

Elizabeth once cared MORE about what others thought about her than about how she felt.
So, whenever she felt bored or sad or alone she'd often reach for comfort food to fill the space.

NOW she does things a whole lot differently.

Be like Elizabeth.

Fill yourself up instead …
…
…
…

with LAUGHTER
with FUN
with MEANINGFUL CONVERSATIONS
with UPLIFTING STORIES
with WALKS ON THE BEACH
with LOVE and APPRECIATION …
…
…
…
…
…
…
…
…
…
…
…

and AN ENTIRE ROOM FULL OF SHOES ☺

CONFESSION #999 ...

I'M REDEFINING WHO I AM

No longer will I define myself by dress size, by money in the bank, by relationship status or even by the way I feel.

I am either,

"Lit Up" or "Getting Ready To Shine".

Both are equally glorious states of being, without needing to achieve anything different to where I currently stand.

CONFESSION #1000 …

TODAY IS THE FIRST DAY OF A BRAND NEW JOURNEY

Where I leave behind all unpleasant experiences from the past, pack and carry the memories I fondly cherish, make peace with what's happening in the present and decide which adventures I'll take in the future. No drama, no explanation, no more story to justify where I've come from, just a gentle moving towards something so much better.

THANK YOU

Thank you for the goodness in front of us.
Thank you for the friends beside us.
Thank you for the roof that shelters us.
Thank you for the love circulating in, through and all around us.
Thank you for the passion that propels us.
Thank you for the joy that exudes from us.
Thank you for the peace that abides in us.
Thank you for the abundance that's gifted to us.
Thank you for the food that nourishes us.
Thank you for the choices that excite us.
Thank you for the air and water that sustains us.
Thank you for incredible bodies that continue to adapt in spite of us.
Thank you for thoughts that encourage us.
Thank you for words that soothe us.
Thank you for actions that value, cherish and acknowledge us.
Thank you for relationships which nurture, comfort and move us.
Thank you for the animals that balance us.
Thank you for the natural world that surrounds us.

Thank you for the people who really care about us.
Thank you for death which provides instant relief for us.
Thank you for the fun that explodes in us.
Thank you for the opportunities that are attracted to us.
Thank you for the desires that are strong in us.
Thank you for the creations that manifest because of us.
Thank you for beliefs that uplift us.
Thank you for our emotions that firmly guide us.
Thank you for the flow of Universal Energy that replenishes us.
Thank you for Infinite Intelligence that's inspired though us.
Thank you for the contrasting experiences that expand us.
Thank you for Divine Life that effortlessly breathes us.
Thank you for the Grace that showers over us.
Thank you for everything that's so readily available to restore us, enhance us and truly empower us. – ER February 2017

To be continued …

"I did it my way, and I wouldn't change a thing."

Note from the Author

Thank you so much for coming along and sharing your time with me. If you enjoyed a few laughs, discovered something new, received insights or found value from any of the Confessions in this book, don't keep it a secret, please take a moment to write a short review so others can find it too. It is greatly appreciated.

Elizabeth Richardson

https://confessions.elizabethrichardson.info
https://amazon.com/author/elizabethrichardson

www.ingramcontent.com/pod-product-compliance
Lightning Source LLC
Chambersburg PA
CBHW071055230426
43666CB00009B/1720